A
ROCK
GUITAR
INSTRUCTION
MANUAL

WRITTEN AND
ILLUSTRATED
BY

RICHARD DANIELS

The capital letters used on the cover and for headings throughout the book are known as the *Capitalis Romana* which were originally inscribed on the Trajan Column, Rome, 114 A.D. This alphabet is regarded as the best basic form in the evolution of letters and is justly known as the most beautiful of all Roman letters. The frontispiece and other elaborate artwork and borders were redrawn from 15th century bibles. The text of the book is set in 11 point Garamond medium.

The hand illustrations were created by photographing Richard's hand on the fretboard of his late model Flying V using slide film. The pictures were then drawn using a slide projector. The Flying V was also used for the pictures of the guitar's hardware in the first chapter. A oo point technical pen was used for all line drawings and graphs in the book.

With the exception of one medieval woodcut print, all diagrams, hand illustrations, transcriptions, lettering layout, technical drawings, and illustrative artwork were created by the author.

Distributed By

Cherry Lane Music Co., inc.
"quality in printed music"

P.O. BOX 430 • PORT CHESTER, NY 10573

Library of Congress Catalog Card Number 78-75075

I.S.B.N. # 0-89524-066-1

Richard P. Daniels is the owner and operator of The Heavy Guitar Company

Layout artist, design consultant—Gil Johnson

CONTENTS

ROADMAP
To The Heavy Guitar Bible

It is easy to get into the Heavy Guitar Bible, just start at the beginning and read. At the end of Chapter One get out your guitar and prepare yourself for some concentrated work. The fretboard, as seen by the rock guitarist, will clearly unfold as we progress with each new chapter.

The Heavy Guitar Bible employs three basic systems to organize and convey technical information. They are used both independently and in conjunction with each other throughout the book.

Diagrams

All diagrams are numbered in sequence and the majority of the diagrams are fretboard representations. However, all graphs and charts are also numbered diagrams, as shown on page 16.

Diagram 36   Blues and relative notes used in transcription–Key of E

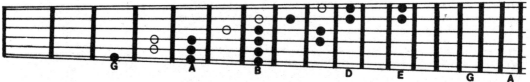

Transcriptions

A six line staff is used for all transcriptions to present musical passages for guitarwork. Along with the sequence number, the key in which the passage takes place is also identified. For complete information, see the six line staff insert after Chapter Three on page 29.

Transcription 5

Hand Illustrations

A variety of fingering techniques are displayed in a series of numbered hand illustrations. The symbols and numbers used on the drawings are explained with the first example on page 23.

Hand Illustration 9

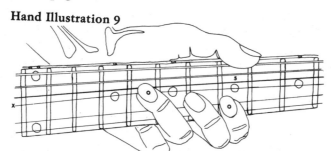

There are 98 diagrams, 88 transcriptions, 28 hand illustrations and also 40 chord figures.

1
EQUIPMENT

The electric guitar is an invention brought about by the new electronics of a technical age. Leaving the tradition of the acoustic guitar far behind, the electric guitar quickly evolved to its present state by adapting any new innovation that gave greater control of the music through electronics. If a new idea created a greater diversity in the sound of the instrument, it was quickly incorporated into the design. The creative electric guitarists of the late sixties proved the electric guitar to be the most versatile of all instruments. Thin steel strings placed over sensitive pickups allowed a control and ease of playing that had never been known before to any musician. The ability to sling the guitar over the shoulder and plug it into an amplifier gave almost complete freedom of movement for stage performance.

An acoustic guitar extracts the energy from the vibrating string to make its own sound, causing the string vibrations to quickly die down, thereby greatly reducing its ability to sustain a note. However, when electronic amplification is added, sound waves from the speakers get back to the guitar and reinforce the strings' vibration and its capability to sustain.

There are basically three different kinds of electric guitars: solid body, hollow body and semi-hollow body. The advantages of the solid body are greater adaptability to electronics, durability and superior treble response. The solid body guitar is strictly electrical although various types of woods and steel reinforcement affect the guitar's ability to sustain.

The hollow body guitar evolved directly from the acoustic guitar and contains its basic design properties: arched sides and back, hollow body cavity, and f-shaped sound holes. Jazz guitarists use hollow body electrics for that subtle, mellow sound created by the resonance of the guitar's body.

The semi-hollow body guitar combines the characteristics of both the solid body and the hollow body guitar into an instrument that is ideal for the rock guitarist concerned with volume levels, sustain and a pure tone. The semi-hollow body guitars have a small body cavity and greater sustain and resonance capability than the solid bodies. They can handle a greater volume level than hollow bodies without creating harsh feedback squeal.

Pot

All high quality electric guitars have at least two pickups and many have three. As a rule, each pickup has its own tone and volume controls, or pots. Most multiple-pickup guitars have a three-position toggle switch which allows different combinations of pickups to be used. Almost all of the hardware on the electric guitar is replaceable with custom pieces, each offering a different design. You can choose exactly the accessories that you want from the tuning keys down to the vibrato tailpiece. High quality replacement pickups are available in good music stores.

The character of a guitar is determined by its body design, craftsmanship, the quality of its electrical equipment and the *string-action* on the neck of the guitar. It is crucial that your guitar has a string action that is compatible with your type of playing. The three variables that determine the string action of a guitar are the frets, the strings and the mechanical adjustments.

Frets

Guitar frets vary between the two extremes of *rounded* and *flat*. The rounded fret is higher so that there is a greater distance between the top of the fret and the wood of the fingerboard. The string action on the rounded fret neck is a little

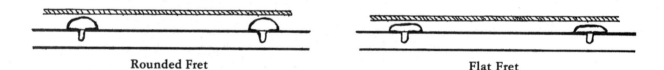

Rounded Fret   Flat Fret

slower than the flat fret, but the fingering is more definite. The added height creates a better condition to grab and hold a note. This type of action allows a greater degree of control for the vibrato technique when the finger is rocked on the string.

Advantages of the flat fret are increased speed and ease of playing. Because the top of the fret is close to the fretboard, all six strings can be adjusted closer to the neck. Many artists have complained that flat fretted guitars do not offer enough control over the playing action.

An additional variable concerning the guitar neck is the degree to which the fingerboard and frets are arched across the neck.

Arched Fretboard   Flat Fretboard

2

Strings

There are many types and sizes of guitar strings. In a set of strings, the first two strings and usually the third are smooth strands of steel. These are the E,B, and G strings. The other three strings, those of lower tones, are wound strings. The core of the wound strings is an alloy of copper, nickle, iron and manganese. This core has a winding around it of fine round wire that is magnetically responsive. Nickle, stainless steel and several alloys are used for the winding.

Wound strings are commonly referred to as unpolished or *round wound* strings and are the most widely used type of string for both rock and folk guitar. *Ground wound* strings are first round wound and then polished with an abrasive to give a smooth, light feel. *Flatwound* strings are wrapped with a flat band of wire which gives the string a very smooth fast feel. Relative to a new set of round wound, the flatwound and ground wound strings have less sustain and produce a more subdued sound.

There is a lot of confusion surrounding the subject of string gauge. Let's consider the variables. Lighter strings are easier to fret and bend for all sorts of lead guitar techniques. The problem is that the lighter the string, the more sustain and resonant quality is sacrificed. Many guitarists complain that they can't grab and hold a note using very thin strings. Thicker strings stay in tune longer, break less frequently and give a fuller ringing sound but are difficult to play fast or bend for lead guitar work. With experimentation, you can find what you need. The following gauge chart covers the spectrum from light to heavy.

String Gauge Chart

	1	2	3	4	5	6
Very Light	.008	.011	.014	.022	.030	.039
Light	.011	.015	.023	.030	.042	.052
Medium	.013	.017	.026	.034	.045	.054
Heavy	.014	.018	.028	.040	.050	.060

Rhythm guitarists generally use thicker strings because they produce a full resonant sound and string bending is usually not required. Lead guitarists usually buy the thickest string which will allow them good control over fretting and technique. Guitarists who make a living with their axes know exactly what gauge string they want on each of their guitars.

Better music stores have special string displays that allow you to buy each string in the desired gauge. Many string companies sell composite string sets which use the top three strings of a very light set and the bottom three strings from a light set (.008, .011, .016, .028, .042, .052). This is a great setup for a lead guitar. Replace strings frequently or you will have trouble tuning your guitar and getting the clear crisp sound that you want.

Mechanical Adjustments

In order to keep your instrument in playing condition, you must be familiar with the mechanical adjustments that can be made to the neck and strings.

Truss Rod Neck Adjustment

The truss rod is located in the neck of the guitar and has an adjustment screw nut which controls the straightness of the neck. The truss rod has one optimum adjustment. This adjustment can be made and explained to you in a good local

Cutaway View of the Neck Showing the Truss Rod

repair shop and is mentioned in most new guitar warranties. The adjustment screw nut is usually located at the top of the neck near the tuning keys and is hidden by a small plastic cover that is easily removed. Unless you have the correct tools and the experience, don't try to adjust the truss rod yourself. A preliminary test for the straightness of the neck can be made by simply looking down the neck from the top of the guitar. If you find that your string height has changed or if any strings buzz above a certain fret, your guitar may need readjustment. Take the guitar to a competent guitar shop.

Plastic cover

Height of Strings above the Fretboard

The adjustment of the up and down movement of the bridge is the easiest adjustment to make and determines the height of the strings above the lower end of the fretboard. Most bridges are designed with two turning adjustments located approximately under the first and sixth strings (see bridge illustration). This facilitates up and down adjustment of all six strings simultaneously. It also allows either side of the bridge to be lowered or raised individually. Experiment with the bridge to find out which height adjustment is best for you. Each time the bridge height is changed the guitar must be retuned.

At the top of the fretboard before the strings attach to the tuning keys, the strings pass over a small strip of plastic or other material which is called a *nut*. The nut is grooved to accept each string and the depth of each groove determines the height of each string at this position. This is an important, essentially permanent adjustment and you should be aware that it can be changed if a change would favor your technique.

Adjustment of String Length

Individual string adjustment on the bridge allows the exact adjustment of string length between the nut at the top of the fretboard and the bridge. This adjustment is made by turning small screws located on the six mini-bridges contained in the main bridge (see bridge illustration). The first harmonic of the open string (which is also the octave) is used as a way of getting each string in perfect adjustment. The first harmonic of a string is sounded by lightly touching (not fretting) any string at the octave (twelfth fret) and plucking it while removing the finger from the string. The resulting pitch is the first harmonic which is ideally matched to the pitch of the string when it is fretted at the twelfth fret. If the two notes are not exactly the same, you either need new strings, a bridge adjustment, or both.

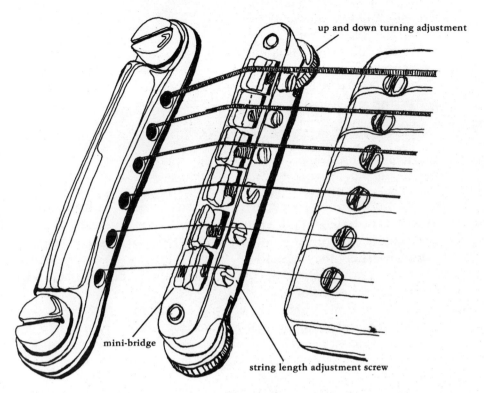

up and down turning adjustment

mini-bridge

string length adjustment screw

The Bridge

Another quick way to determine correct string adjustment is to play the open string and then to play the same string fretted at the octave. If it fails to sound a perfect octave, it is not in good adjustment. Have a guitar technician show you how to make the correcting adjustment.

Pickups

A transducer converts energy from one form to another. A pickup is an electromechanical transducer which converts the tones produced by string vibrations into impulses of electricity. The frequency of the electric impulses correspond to the frequency of the vibrating string.

The first guitar pickups, those used in the 20's and 30's, were simple crystal or dynamic contact microphones. Modern pickups are made of an oblong permanent magnet and six magnetically charged polepieces surrounded by a coil formed by thousands of wraps of very thin wire, about .0026" in diameter. A polepiece is positioned directly under each of the strings. The vibration of the strings in the magnetic field generates corresponding currents of electricity in the coil.

The properties of string vibration are complex. Stretched taut between the nut and the bridge, the string produces lower frequencies near the middle of the string and higher, treble frequencies near either end. There is usually no structural difference between a guitar's pickups, but the term bass pickup indicates placement in the guitar body near the end of the fretboard. The treble pickup is located near the bridge.

Pickups are generally divided into two groups: the *single coil* variety, which are older and have been used for decades on the Fender Telecaster and Stratocaster,

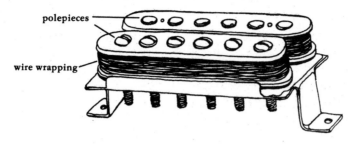

polepieces

wire wrapping

Double Coil Humbucking Pickup

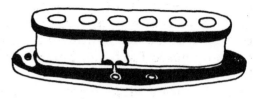

Single Coil Pickup

and the *double coil* humbucking pickup which was first used on Gibson guitars. The single coil pickup is noted for its super bright treble reproduction. The two coils of the humbucking are placed side by side and wired in series, so the electricity passes through one then the other, and out of phase so the current flows in opposite directions through the two coils. This unique design cancels opposing electrical hum created by either coil.

Modern pickups employ either of two types of magnetic materials: a special metal alloy, alnico, composed of aluminum, nickle, and cobalt, or ceramic, which is impregnated with iron particles. Ceramic magnets are more resistant to demagnification, are more powerful than the alloy type and are commonly denoted by the letters ox in the brand name.

Most pickups have six small cylindrical magnets or polepieces. These protrude through the pickup cover and are often threaded to allow individual adjustment to each string. Some polepieces simply conduct magnetism from the centrally located magnet (humbucking) while in other pickups the polepieces are magnets (single coil telecaster). Electrical response increases as the polepiece is adjusted closer to the string, but if they are too close, magnetic string distortion occurs.

The strength of a pickup's output is determined primarily by the power of the magnet and the number of wraps in the coils. The more wraps of wire, the stronger the output signal of the pickup. The pickup's output is measured in ohms (abbreviated Z) which is the resistance to current flow. *Low impedance* pickups have fewer wraps of wire and are usually rated below 600 ohms. Practically all pickups sold are *high impedance* and are rated at 8,000 ohms or greater. One of the problems encountered by the designers of "hot" or high output pickups is that as the number of wraps is increased, there is a loss of treble. So there is a compromise between frequency response and total pickup output. Low impedance pickups require a transformer to boost the low output signal before reaching the amp. Low impedance pickups have a cleaner sound, greater frequency response and can be used with a longer cord without electrical interference, unlike the high impedance units where every foot of cord adds capacitance or stored electricity which causes hum and frequency response loss. Practically all studio guitarists use low impedance equipment (e.g. the Les Paul Recording, Professional and Signature are all low impedance guitars), but if you use hot pickups to get sustain and gut power, buy a high quality shielded cord which is as short as possible for your purposes.

A phase switch is an inexpensive sound modification which allows the guitarist to get a funky, snarling blues sound from his axe. A bipolar switch is wired to reverse two pickups' phase relationship by running the pickups live wire to the ground. The resulting tone is a sweet harmonic "squeak" which can also be

6

obtained from a picking technique where the tip of the thumb mutes the ringing string immediately after the pick.

FM radio transmitters are now available to those lucky rock stars who can afford them. A mini FM transmitter at the guitar broadcasts the signal from the pickups over an unused FM band. The receiver is usually located at the group's control board which sends the signal back through the speakers of the P.A. or the guitar amp. No messy wires to get in star's way.

Guitars

Of all six string electric guitars, Gibson guitars are by far the most popular. Gibson is the only company that manufactures a widely accepted full line of guitars for professionals in practically every musical category. If you care to know more about what is presently available to today's guitarists, go to a large music store and ask to see the color catalogue for both Gibson and Fender electric guitars. This will give you a primer for what is going on. There are many great guitar companies who will send you literature upon request. If you are interested in learning about the specifics of guitar construction, the history of Gibson or Fender or other interesting guitar facts, see the Appendix Section, *Other Books.*

The section below is intended to give the basic facts on the rock guitars which are most widely used.

Gibson manufactures many different electric guitars, but the two with the greatest impact on the rock music world are the SG solid body and the Les Paul semi-hollow body.

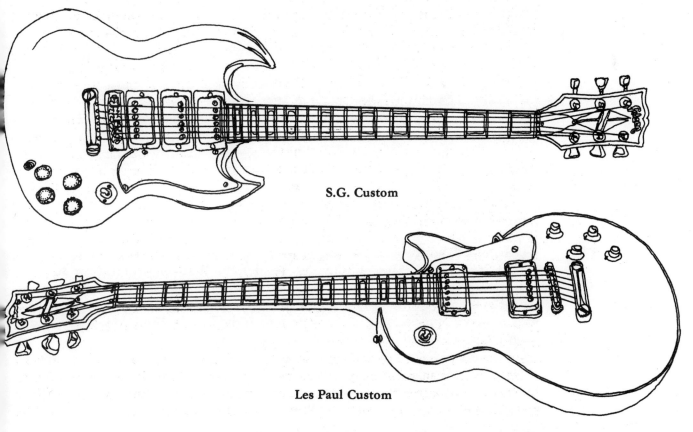

S.G. Custom

Les Paul Custom

There is a very intricate history to both of these guitars. The Les Paul guitar was first introduced in 1952. The S.G. was first produced in 1964. Over the years, special limited editions were issued that offered custom features. There are basically two different kinds of each model. The S.G. Standard has rounded frets and two chrome plated humbucking pickups and the S.G. Custom is available with flat frets and three gold plated humbuckings. The Les Paul Deluxe has rounded frets with two small humbuckings and is available in a number of different colors, including gold, red, blue, and natural wood. The Les Paul Custom is available with flat frets and two (the late fifties models had three) gold plated humbuckings. The flat fretted Les Paul Custom is known as the "Fretless Wonder."

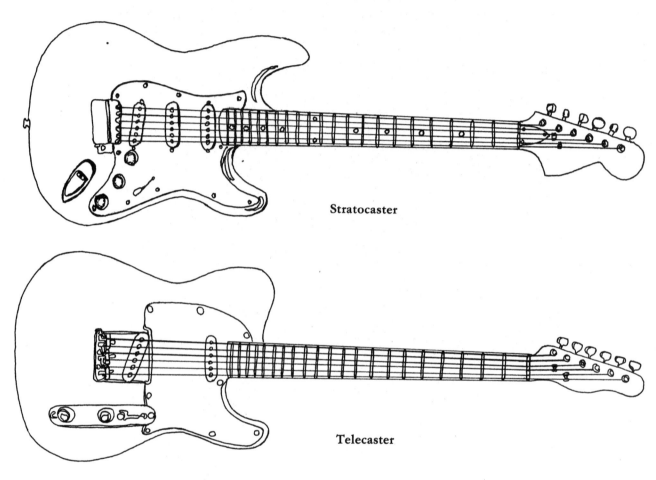

Stratocaster

Telecaster

The single favorite guitar of the whole rock generation, perhaps, is the famous Fender Stratocaster. Designed by Leo Fender and first sold in 1954 for $249.50 with tremolo bar, this great guitar has not changed in basic design. Jimi Hendrix played this semi-rounded fret guitar almost exclusively. The fretboard of the Stratocaster is arched to a greater degree than the Les Paul and S.G. model and is the most widely used guitar which has three single coil pickups.

The Fender Telecaster was introduced in 1948 when it was called the Broadcaster. This single coil double pickup guitar is a classic and was first accepted by the country and western pickers of the fifties. In 1973 the Teledeluxe was introduced with a new sculptured body and two humbucking pickups.

Of course, custom accessories are used by practically all guitar fanatics and they mix and match parts, pieces of hardware and body parts to the degree where almost each old axe has its own special history. Here are the names of a few more Gibson guitars which have made their mark in the world of rock guitar. The Gibson Flying V (used for many illustrations in this book) has a mahogany body which is shaped like an arrowhead, and has been used by Jimi Hendrix, J. Geils and Albert King. The Firebird is a limited edition that has a trapezoidal shaped body with special tuning heads that are designed perpendicular to the body of the guitar. The Firebird is used exclusively by Johnny Winter. The Explorer has the body of an exaggerated Firebird and is often used by Rick Derringer. Old Les Paul Juniors and the Melody Makers were early solid body single pickup guitars that you often see played with two humbuckings intact. The GibsonEW-335 and the ES 345 are both semi-hollow body arch top guitars with large bodies. Chuck Berry, Alvin Lee, and B.B. King have each played one or the other of these two great guitars throughout their careers.

Between Guitar and Amp

In the past few years there have been innumerable gadgets invented to plug in between the guitar and the amp which alter the signal from the pickups before it reaches the amplifier. The possibilities for electronically influencing the guitar's signal have been thoroughly explored because of the demand for unusual sounds. Effective use of such devices means experimentation with all of the various controls on the amp, guitar, and the devices themselves.

The majority of these accessories are packaged in small steel or aluminum boxes designed for floor use with an on-and-off foot switch located on the top. An additional cord is needed for any type of floor device, although several smaller units have been designed to plug directly into the guitar. These sound effect devices use state-of-the-art circuits and can usually be purchased for under $100.00. If you carefully explore the possibilities of an effect box, you can push your music into another dimension simply by stepping on a foot switch.

Sustain and *distortion* are of primary importance to all electric guitarists. The nature of rock music lends itself to the fluid quality of sustain and the coarse distortion of high volume. The greatest advantage of distortion devices is their ability to produce the "dirty" overdriven sound of tube amps at a low volume level. Distortion devices work best with single note leads and single chords.

The common fuzz tone is familiar to most rock guitarists. It creates controlled harmonic overload by amplifying the incoming signal from the guitar cord with a battery and other circuits. If close attention is not given to the controls on the amp and the guitar, the fuzz tone can sound flat and metallic.

Many of the devices for sale are simple *boosters* which take the signal from the guitar and amplify either the treble or the bass. They act as a mini pre-amp which enlarges a certain part of the signal.

Some of the sounds created by the various devices were inspired by sounds that are naturally acoustic. The incredible *wa wa* pedal is modeled after the sound of a muted trumpet and can be oscillated with the use of a variable position foot pedal. Many such pedals serve as a variable volume device when the *wa wa* is switched off. An *envelope follower* produces a triggered or touch controlled wa which is activated by the incoming signal.

The *phase shifter* employs electrical circuitry to simulate the sound of the Lesley Cabinet originally used for organs. The Lesley Cabinet has revolving speaker horns and, as it turns, the wavelengths have a mesmerizing effect upon the listener. A *flanger* is a device related to the shifter because it produces the swirling sound of revolving speakers but with a more intense, flowing, musical sound. The *echo* device produces a discreet repetition of the guitar's pickup signal which occurs immediately after the original playing. There are several different types of echo machines using a wide variety of technology to create the repeated signal. The analog delay models are the cheapest and use only circuitry to reproduce the signal. Tape models use a tape loop and several playback heads to replay the original signal. The speed at which the tape loop is run past the playback heads determines the interval of the echo. Quality recording studios have special echo machines which are capable of duplicating an input signal within a few milliseconds creating an effect called doubling or thickening.

Reverb and *tremolo* are usually built into modern guitar amps. A tremolo unit uniformly oscillates the incoming signal at a set interval which is regulated by speed and intensity controls. A reverberation unit simulates the sound of an amplifier being played in a large auditorium.

Many of the new innovative devices differ from standard devices because they differentiate frequencies rather than accept the incoming signal as complete. An example of this is the *equalizer* which changes the tone of a sound by boosting selected frequencies between treble and bass by channeling separate divisions of the spectrum through a corresponding series of manual controls called bands.

Another common electronic technique is to receive incoming wavelengths and produce new notes which are mathematically related to the notes being played. An *Octave Divider* provides a note which is one octave lower than the one being played. An *Octave Multiplier* forms notes an octave above the original note. A *Ring Modulator* makes gong-like or bell tones which are related to the original notes being played.

Musical synthesizers are sophisticated studio networks which use this related wavelength principle to produce an entire spectrum of effects which include multiple octave duplication. The effects produced by today's complex synthesizers would astonish studio producers of the 1950's. The capabilities of synthesizers vary widely according to the number of component functions or *patches* designed into the unit. Ring modulators, wa wa's and envelope followers are standard subsystems of any quality synthesizer.

A *Compressor* is a device used on stage and in practically every recording studio. Compressors allow an individual musician to be heard without over-powering the other members of the group by sending the guitar's signal through an adjustable preset loudness control which boosts lows and reduces highs to fit into a desired range creating a clean sustaining sound. *Limiting* works on the same principle except it only handles the high volume range.

A *noise gate* is a device which works on the incoming electrical signal, eliminating the lower end of the noise frequencies which contain most of the hum and electrical noise produced by added circuitry.

Hard wired is a term used to indicate that an effect device or any added circuitry has been wired in such a way that the basic line between guitar and amp is wired directly past all circuits in the device when not in use (switched off) as if it were not on the line. Even when standard devices are switched off there is still a flow of electricity through a few of the circuits.

Amplifiers

The amplifier takes the signal from the guitar, feeds it into a *pre-amp* (quality amps have several pre-amp stages), then refines the signal with tone controls or whatever accessories are built into the amp such as reverb or boosters. The signal then goes through a *driver stage* which further conditions it for input to the *power amp* after which it is transmitted to the speakers.

There are two different kinds of basic amplifiers: *tube models* and *solid state,* which are the center of controversy wherever amps are used. The usual questions are: What's the difference? Which is better?

The solid state amp has its advantages: it is more resistant to vibration and heat and may operate indefinitely without the replacement of parts. It has an overall smaller physical size, turns on instantly and is lighter in weight than tube amps. Solid state amps are also noted for a greater efficiency ratio of watts-in to watts-out from power plug to power output. Most transistor amps have protective circuits to avoid overload conditions. These amps produce low impedance output which enables them to be directly coupled to standard low impedance speakers. Speakers driven by a solid state amp have a higher damping factor, which means that the speaker cone quickly returns to its normal position after each movement. This gives transistor amps a clear, crisp, sound reproduction.

Tube amps have been around as long as guitar amplifiers and employ easily replaceable tubes. Pre-amp tubes have a longer life than power amp tubes. Tube amps produce high impedance signals which require a transformer to lower the impedance to the standards of common speakers. The output transformer is precisely the stage that is responsible for the distinctive sound of tube amps.

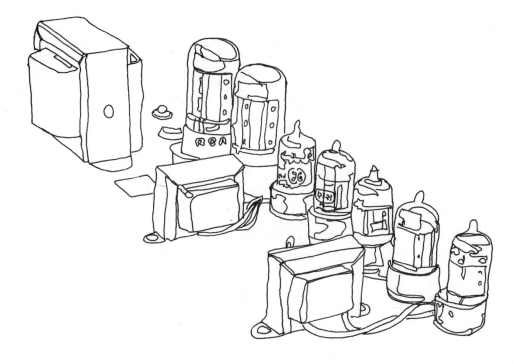

Harmonic distortion, sustain and that real "live" sound have traditionally been the trademark of the tube amp and because of these qualities, many true rockers will have no part of solid state amps. Tube amps can produce a controlled sustain and feedback when at the same volume the solid state amp will squeal with a sharp uncontrollable treble sound. Nevertheless, the solid state amp has its place in many different types of guitar music. In a recording studio, with the use of effect devices and the amps set at half volume, it may make little difference if the amp is tube or solid state, but on stage or jamming live, the tube amp will give you that gut distortion that you hear on the first album of the Jimi Hendrix Experience or Led Zeppelin.

In an attempt to reproduce the characteristic tube sound, many solid state amps now contain modified preamps, master volume controls (explained below) or built-in fuzz devices. Many new amps contain both a solid state preamp and a tube power supply with an output transformer.

The single most confusing aspect of amplifier specification is the power or watt rating. Let's clear up one small point first: The *draw* of an amplifier is the amount of wattage that it takes out of the wall socket. The *output* is the wattage delivered to the speakers by the amplifier. If you are considering buying a particular amplifier, don't become confused by the indescriminate use of the words *watt* or *wattage*. There are five different methods for measuring an amplifier's output, all of which have their own names: *RMS, Peak, music power, peak music* and *instantaneous peak power*. RMS, *Root Mean Square,* is really the only one to use because it is a measurement of how the amplifier can regularly deliver power. The other ratings can be as much as ten times higher than RMS so...watch out!

When buying an amplifier, the size and the power of the amp that you need depends on two things: the size and the power of the equipment of your fellow musicians and the size of the room in which you will be playing. If possible, use the amp that you want to buy with the musicians you'll be playing with, preferably in the actual playing situation.

Speakers and Enclosures

A speaker functions in quite the opposite manner than a pickup. The pulses of electrical energy produced by the amp activiates an electromagnet (a voice coil) behind the apex of the speaker cone which is connected to a large magnet bar constructed behind the coil. Ultimately, this moves the paper speaker cone rapidly back and forth, vibrating in frequency with the pulses of electrical energy. The air in front of the speaker similarly vibrates to produce audible sound waves.

The size of a speaker may mean little when it comes to total sound and power. One twelve inch speaker can vary in wattage capacity from 20 to 200 watts. The higher the wattage capacity, the larger the magnet will be on the back of the speaker. The larger the voice coil the higher the efficiency.

There are two different systems used for containing the complete guitar amplification system. One is a self-contained unit with the amp and the speakers in the same enclosure. The second system divides the amp and speakers into two different enclosures. The smaller self-contained units are more portable, however, the two-component system separates the amp from the speaker vibration, can be used while the components are separated and can be mixed and matched. The double cabinet system caught on in the sixties as the demand for larger amps made the single unit too cumbersome.

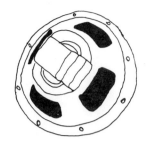

When the amplifier became separate from the speakers, a lot more attention was focused on the design of speaker cabinets. *Finite baffle* enclosures have open backs delivering speaker projection from both the front and the rear. Practically all self-contained amps with two twelves or under are in this category. *Infinite baffle* enclosures are sealed tight on all six sides, with the speakers securely mounted over their circular mounting ports. This method limits cone movement but improves bass frequency response. The *bass reflex* cabinet has openings of a calculated dimension called ports which are mathematically tuned to both cabinet and speaker size. A well designed bass reflex enclosure can greatly increase a speaker's mechanical and acoustical performance.

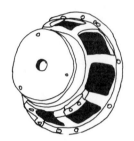

You can save yourself a lot of trouble if you take note of a few key points before you hook up any combination of speakers and amplifiers. First check that the wattage requirements of the speakers are not less than the wattage you are using to drive them. If you are wiring up more than one speaker you must consider whether the speakers are in *phase*. This is done by making sure that all speaker wire terminals are receiving the correct connection, either ground or live. Phasing can be checked while you are taking care of the *impedance match* between amp and speakers. Multispeaker amplifiers can be wired for impedance in one of three ways: series, parallel and series/parallel. Discuss the possibilities with your local amp repair shop. Before you drive all the way down there, write down the impedance specifications of your amp (is it variable?) along with the number of speakers involved and their ohm rating.

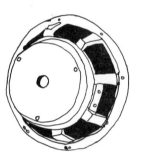

The Small Amp and the Stage

The overall concept design of the smaller self-contained guitar amps has greatly improved in the last few years. When the big rock groups started to form in the late sixties, each musician in the group had his own amp and if the sound of the band got louder, each musician had to buy larger and larger amps for his own use. The P.A. system now plays an important part in the total sound output of the rock band. The amp of each musician is monitored by a microphone placed directly in front of the amp pointing at the speakers. These lines from the stage mikes are then bound together and run to the main control board which is operated by a technician who sits near the back of the auditorium. The sound of each instrument is balanced and then run through the powerful P.A. system. Rather than trying to fill the auditorium with the sound from his own amp, the guitarist can concentrate on the sound he wants out of his amp and let the sound man in the crowd establish the balance between the different instruments and voices. The small amp has been developed for a total sound to be reamplified through the P.A. system. The band members hear the P.A. system through a subsystem containing stage monitors which are speakers placed on the front of the stage facing the performer. For recording purposes, a monitor line is often obtained by running a line directly out of the back of the guitar amps.

The small amp with one or two high quality 12-inch speakers has been used for many of rock and roll's greatest moments. In the studio, it is often the single twelve inch speaker tube amp, turned up to capacity, that produces the incredible roaring sustain and feedback that sounds like a wall of amplifiers when played back on a record player.

Many artists that find the fuzz tone lacking in certain essentials have discovered that the small amp, approaching full power, produces distortion naturally using the unaltered signal straight from the guitar.

One of the greatest innovations designed into many of the new powerful breed of small amps is the *master volume control.* This is a device located in between the pre-amp and the driver stage that permits the regular volume knob to be turned up overdriving the pre-amp to create distortion. The master volume then controls the actual volume so distorted tones can be created at very low volume levels. There is usually a safety switch which is turned on before the master volume is used. This protects component parts from a drastic overload.

The *polarity switch* on an amplifier changes the direction of the current into the amp. If you get a slight shock from touching another person's equipment or microphone, you need to have the polarity of your amplifier reversed. If you do not have a two-way polarity switch on your amp, simply unplug your amp from the wall, turn the plug around one half-turn, and plug it back in.

The term clipping refers to amplifier overload. The amplifier cannot cope with the distorted signal that it is producing and when this overload hits the speakers it can cause a painful screech and destroy the speakers. Turn the amp off—quick!!

Heavy Vibes

Did you ever really think about it—this whole thing is a study from micro to macro and everything in between. Thin metal strings stretched between two points. The initial vibration chain is created when the plastic comes off the strings. Electrons in a current within a magnetic field are a shadow image of the real air vibes; refined and phased, wa waed and boosted, fuzzed and divided. Once the message hits the big generators, all hell breaks loose. Billions of excited electrons have joined the troops, moving against each other, yet remembering to hold the patterned code. One more mirror image magnet trick and we're back to real air vibrations.

2 BASICS

A certain amount of musical theory should be understood before the possibilities of the guitar are explored. The purpose of this chapter is to present the standard musical information that you will need to work with the guitar fretboard and to talk and interact with other musicians.

A sound is generated on the guitar by the vibration of an elastic string which is characterized by its *frequency* (number of vibrations per second) and its *amplitude* (height of the soundwave), and these two characteristics determine the pitch and loudness of the sound. Early scientists discovered that soundwaves can be classified by frequency into strict mathematical categories similar to those used to measure light phenomenon and wave movement through solids and liquids.

The Octave

The range of human hearing is limited to a spectrum of frequencies. An octave is a measurement of sound within this limited range. According to the formal definition, an octave is composed of eight "diatonic" notes. However, as anybody can see from the piano keyboard, the octave is actually composed of twelve half notes which include all white and black keys. Just as a twelve inch ruler can measure heights of over one foot, the octave repeats itself over and over again using the same named notes (A,B,C,D...). It is possible for the same named notes to appear in different octaves because each note has a different frequency and multiples of that frequency produce the same named note in different octaves.

The word *sharp* means simply one note above and is designated by this symbol #. The word *flat* means one note below and is designated by this symbol ♭. The words sharp and flat are also used in describing the pitch of a string during the tuning of the guitar. If a string is sharp then it is tuned too high, if it is flat, it is too low.

The piano is a good visual example of how the octave repeats itself. Diagram 1 illustrates the twelve notes of the octave on the keyboard.

15

Diagram 1 The keyboard with letter name notes

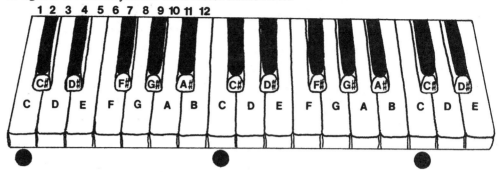

The seven white keys are the notes A through G.
The five black keys are the sharps of the notes A, C, D, F and G.

There is no sharp or flat between the letter notes B and C or between E and F. On the piano these are the two sets of white notes that are side by side that are not divided by a black key. Because there are no sharps or flats between these sets of notes, an E sharp is the same as an F note and a C flat is a B note. For this reason you will rarely hear of an E sharp, F flat, B sharp or C flat. With the exception of these two pairs of notes, there is a sharp or flat between the other letter notes. A *whole step* is a musical reference meaning two notes above any given note in the twelve note progression of the octave. For instance, A is a whole step above G. On the guitar a *whole step* is *two frets* and a *half step* is *one fret*.

The Fretboard

The invention of the fret enabled the musican to "fix" a string at a definite pitch simply by pressing it to the fingerboard. The musical possibilities of a fretted instrument are, in many ways, greater than those instruments designed to play one note at a time, for example, the saxaphone or the flute.

Diagram 2 Notes on low E string and keyboard

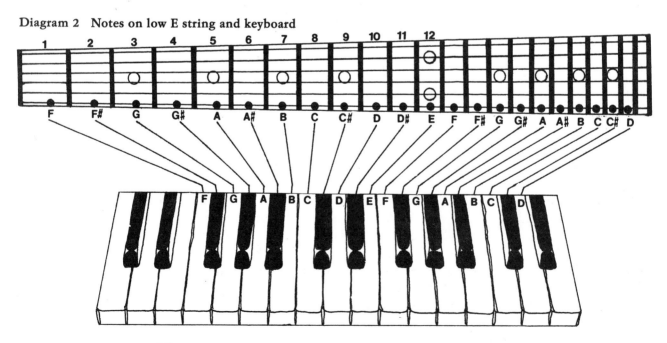

16

Most of today's six string electric guitars have twenty-two frets. The sixth string (thickest string) is tuned to an E note and is called the low E string. The diagram above shows the notes on the low E string as they relate to the piano keyboard.

This string sounds an E note when it is plucked open (no fretting) and each fret above the open string represents the next note in the twelve note octave. Fingering the E string at the fifth fret produces an A note, at the tenth fret, a D note. The twelfth fret is the octave of the open E note and is usually designated by a double dot on the fretboard at this fret. Above this mark the octave repeats itself again. The F note found on the thirteenth fret of this string is the octave of the F note sounded on the first fret.

Diagram 3   Notes on the first twelve frets of the fingerboard

E	F	F#	G	G#	A	A#	B	C	C#	D	D#	E
B	C	C#	D	D#	E	F	F#	G	G#	A	A#	B
G	G#	A	A#	B	C	C#	D	D#	E	F	F#	G
D	D#	E	F	F#	G	G#	A	A#	B	C	C#	D
A	A#	B	C	C#	D	D#	E	F	F#	G	G#	A
E	F	F#	G	G#	A	A#	B	C	C#	D	D#	E

The second string of the guitar is tuned to an A note and is smaller in diameter than the E String. The A note sounded by this open string is the same note played by the E string at the fifth fret. If the E string were permanently depressed at the fifth fret, it would play an open A note. The B note played on the seventh fret of the E string is the same note played on the second fret of the A string.

It is in this way, the transferring of the notes to a smaller higher pitched string, that the six strings carry the continuum of the octaves up the fretboard. The notes of the open strings are as follows:

Diagram 4

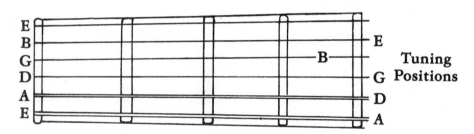

Open String Letter Names

E B G D A E

Tuning Positions

E B G D A

Tuning

The tuning of the guitar starts with the tuning of the low E string to the proper E note on a piano or tuning flute. The A string is then tuned to the A note played on the fifth fret of the low E string. Each string is tuned to the note played on the fifth fret of the thicker string immediately below it with the exception of the second string which is tuned to the third string at the fourth fret.

Another method for tuning the guitar uses harmonics or overtones common to the vibrating string. The fundamental frequency results from playing the open string. The other harmonic wavelengths are simple multiples of the fundamental (¼, ½, etc.). The first harmonic divides the string length into two equal parts with the half way mark exactly over the octave at the twelfth fret. In order to sound the harmonic tone, lightly touch (do not fret) the string over the designated fret and pluck while removing the finger. The *second harmonic* divides the fundamental into thirds and can be sounded at the seventh or nineteenth fret. The *third harmonic* can be sounded at the fifth fret and is precisely one fourth of the fundamental.

For tuning purposes, harmonics are used in this way: sound the third harmonic at the *fifth fret* on the low E string letting it ring. Then sound the second harmonic at the *seventh fret* on the A string and tune this string until the resulting pitches are identical. Each string can be tuned in the same way (from lower to higher), with the exception of the B string which is tuned using the fretted note method explained above.

When it comes right down to playing, one of the best ways to tune is directly with the chord. If you are playing a song in the key of A, before you start, strum an A chord. If tuning is needed, finger the chord firmly, strum and make machine head adjustment with the right hand.

Repeating Notes

The first string (thinnest) and the sixth string (thickest) are both E strings. The six strings, when in tune and played open, span two octaves. It is very important to understand this concept because it is the building block for other ideas and musical structures. There is a difference of *two octaves*, twenty-four notes, between the low E and the high E string. As the notes climb from the low E string at the rate of five notes a string, they reach their half-way mark at the end of the first octave. This is an E note, on the second fret of the fourth string (D string).

The high E string then carries the notes up through a third octave to the E note on the twelfth fret. The twenty-second fret on this string is a D note which can be physically pushed sideways across the fretboard to sound a crowning E note. This makes the guitar a four octave instrument compared to the seven and one third octaves of the piano. In the diagram below all of the E notes on the fingerboard have been numbered as they show the progression of the three octaves from the low E to the twelfth fret of the high E string. Notice how the same notes (from the same octave) appear in different positions.

Diagram 5   Repetition of E notes

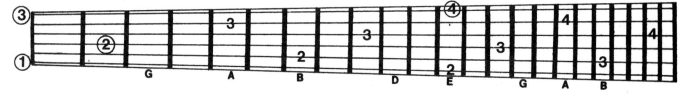

There are actually twelve E notes on the fretboard (two on each string) but eight of these notes repeat one of the original circled E notes that divide the octaves. The E notes are constantly used as reference points for lead work and chord change.

A great deal of rock music is played in the key of A and E because these keys easily lend themselves to the changes of the music. The above example has been given to illustrate the E notes as they appear on the fretboard, but remember that the same mathematical repetition is happening to all of the notes in the octave in the same way.

3
CHORDS
AND
STRUCTURE

Chords are the simultaneous sounding of three or more tones. Chords are constructed using principles involving the major scale which are explained in Chapter 12, *Building.* Along with chord configurations, this chapter explains the use of the *root note* for finding the letter names of chords, illustrates the use of bar chords and explains all of the chords commonly used for a given key. It also demonstrates the twelve and eight bar blues and then explores a few of the dimensions of songwriting. So don't say nobody ever took the time to show it all to you!!

The chords below are those which are most used by electric guitarists. Examples are given for all of the primary categories. However, good chord books are available which diagram hundreds of chords.

Chords

The numbers within the dots on the strings in the chord chart below correspond to the fingers on the left hand: Index–one, Middle–two, Ring–three, Pinky–four. An O means that the string is not played and is usually muted by the thumb or an unused finger. Open strings are played.

E chords – root letter name on sixth or low E string.

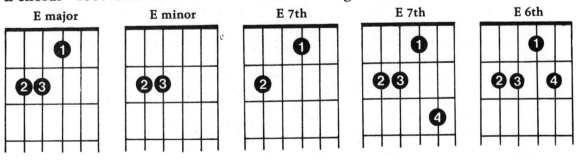

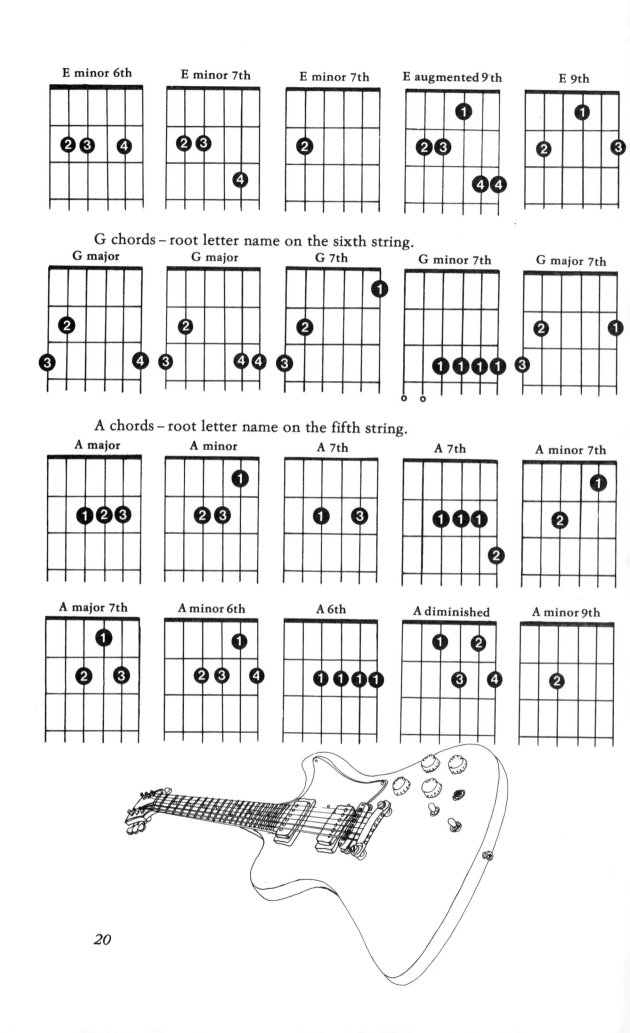

E minor 6th E minor 7th E minor 7th E augmented 9'th E 9th

G chords – root letter name on the sixth string.

G major G major G 7th G minor 7th G major 7th

A chords – root letter name on the fifth string.

A major A minor A 7th A 7th A minor 7th

A major 7th A minor 6th A 6th A diminished A minor 9th

B chords – root letter name on the fifth string.

B major	B minor	B 7th	B minor 7th	B 9th

C chords – root letter name on the fifth string.

C major	C 7th	C major 7th	C 6th	C 9th

D chords – root letter name on the fourth string.
Rounded Fret

D major	D 7th	D minor 7th	D major 7th	D minor

Movable Chords

The following are *movable chords* and they can be played in any vertical position. Study them closely and figure out how they relate to the other basic chords. The circled note designates the note which contains the root note letter name.

The first two movable chords are derived from the G major root chord diagrammed in the G chords section. The third and fourth chords shown are derived from the C seventh chord. The next two chords, both major sevenths, originated from the E major and the D major chord respectively. The following 9th chord is a configuration formed off the root note fret which is explained later in this book. The final three chords were obtained from the basic E major chord which appears at the very beginning of the chart. Of course any part of any bar chord could be considered a movable chord and for full understanding all positions should be explored.

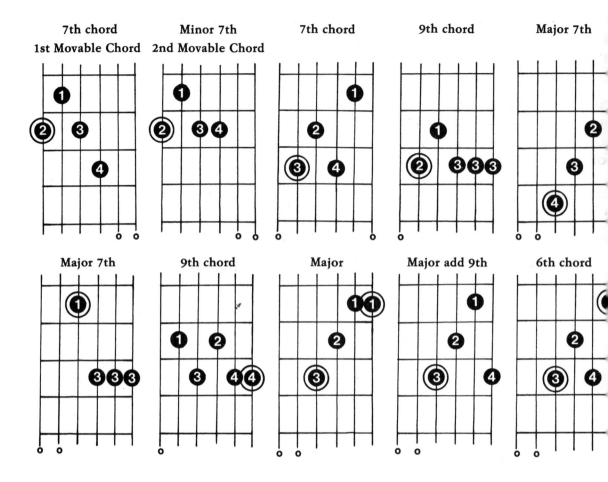

| 7th chord | Minor 7th | 7th chord | 9th chord | Major 7th |
| 1st Movable Chord | 2nd Movable Chord | | | |

| Major 7th | 9th chord | Major | Major add 9th | 6th chord |

Bar Chords

The most important chords in rock music are E and A major because with these chords, *bar* chords can be formed. Bar chords are movable up and down the fretboard, keeping the same fixed finger pattern, but creating different letter name chords at each fret.

This gives the guitarist the option of arranging a sequence of guitar chords in a number of ways. To form a bar chord using the E major chord (see Hand Illustration 1), make the E chord with the last three fingers of the left hand. In order to form a barred G chord, slide the fingers three frets up making sure to keep them in the same pattern, then place the index finger across all of the strings at the third fret.

The last three fingers form the chord in the same pattern that was used to form the E chord at the bottom, starting with open strings. The index finger acts as a bar in the same way that the nut holds the strings stationary at the end of the fretboard for the E major chord. The fret to which you raise the bar (index finger) determines the letter name of the chord. The *chord name* will be the same as the *root note* played by the tip of the index finger on the low E string. For instance, in the above example the G bar chord was formed by placing the index finger across the third fret. In this position the index finger plays a G note on the low E string. This G note is the *root note* for the chord.

The fret which has the bar (index finger) across it is known as the *root note fret*. The root note fret is a very special reference point for the "centering" of all lead guitar patterns.

Bar chords using the A major chord are made in the same way as E major chords except that the root note of the chords is played by the index finger on the A string (Hand Illustration 3). For convenience the ring finger is often used to play the A chord formation across the 2nd, 3rd, and 4th string, while the index plays the fifth string. The low and high E strings are usually muted during A major bar chord formations by the finger forming the bar.

Throughout this book an O appears on the fingernail of the fingers actually used in fretting. An X is placed on each string that is played. Where it is necessary, a number will be placed on the fretboard to designate the root note fret.

Hand Illustration 1 Complete E bar using index finger   Hand Illustration 2 Complete E bar using thumb and index

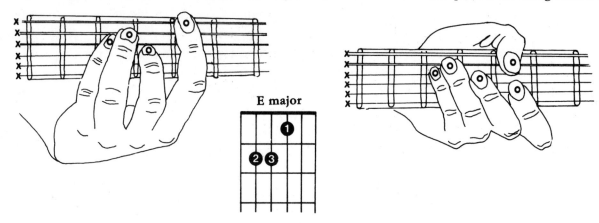

E major

Hand Illustration 3 Complete A bar using index finger   Hand Illustration 4 Complete A bar using thumb and index

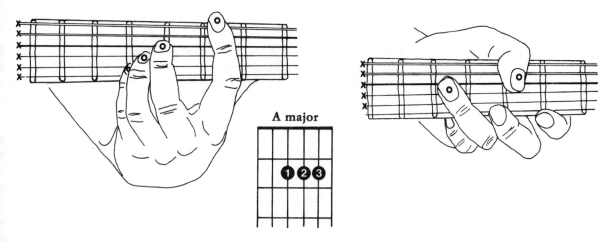

A major

During the formation of bar chords, many artists play the low E string and often the A string with their thumb (see Hand Illustrations 2 and 4). By simply wrapping the thumb around the neck, the E bar can easily be made with the thumb on the low E and the index fretting the two thin strings rather than barring all six. This trick is used for speed and ease of playing and lends itself to playing in a standing position.

Bar chords offer the guitarist a new playing dimension because they can be quickly moved to different positions. The same root chord can be played in various positions, each with a different tonal quality. Many other chords are suitable for barring including the seventh and minor chords of the various major chords.

The movable chords at the bottom of the chord chart are very important for rock guitarists and you should practice substituting them for other common root chords where it is possible.

Chords play a large part in the total understanding of lead guitar. The ability to chord properly and to know where the important bar chords are located can help you play more creatively with a deeper understanding of the fretboard. The scales and patterns that are shown later in this book will work integrally with different chord positions. Your understanding of the relationship between chords and lead guitar scales will determine your ability to freely improvise. Most of Hendrix's lead work, particularly the flowing notes that were used as fillers during the chord changes of a song (*Little Wing* from the album *Bold as Love*), were taken right off the chord. This means that the notes of the chord itself were used in combination with the surrounding notes from special patterns to form complete lead riffs.

For this reason, it is important to take the E and A major chords, their minor chords, etc. and bar them at each fret on the board naming and fretting each one carefully until you are confident about where the chord changes can take place. Initially, the total number and types of chords seem overwhelming, but when you become familiar with the notes on the low E and A string you will find that there are definite limits to the fretboard. There are a limited number of E chords that can be made and in time you will know all of them. Always keep in mind that there is another position in which to play a chord change or riff on the fretboard.

Understanding the Structure of Rock Music

The roots of rock music come from the three chord blues. For this reason, the skeletal chord structure of most rock songs originates from three basic chord changes. If a song is in the key of E, the three common chords that you are most likely to find in the song are:

Diagram 6   The three basic chords to the blues

1st Basic chord	The E chord	The root note chord played with an open E string.
2nd Basic chord	The A chord	Made with an E bar chord at the fifth fret.
3rd Basic chord	The B chord	Made with an E bar chord at the seventh fret.

This example in the key of E presents us with a universal rule. To find the basic chords used in any song, figure out the first basic chord of the key in which the song is being played. Then count five frets above the root note of the first basic chord on the low E string to find the root note for the second basic chord. Then counting seven frets, find the root note of the third basic chord. Applying this to another example in the key of A, the three chords would be; A major, D major and E major.

These three basic chords are also known as the first, fourth and fifth respectively, because of their positional relationship with the seven note major scale (see chapter 11). The first basic chord is technically known as the *tonic or first,* the second basic chord is the *sub-dominant* and the third is the *dominant.*

Here is an arrangement of the twelve notes of the octave that will help you find the three basic chords in any key. It is a helpful tool known as the circle of fifths or the musical wheel.

A   E   B   F#   C#   G#   D#   A#   F   C   G   D   A   E   B   etc.

Pick the letter of the key in which you want to play and the letter to the immediate left will be the second basic chord and the letter to the right will be the third basic chord.

Practically all rock songs use the three basic chords in one way or another. Of course not all songs use the basic chords, but most of the rock music uses these three chords as a base. Through the years, rock musicians have proved the incredible diversity of changes that are possible on these three chords. *Sunshine of Your Love, I Want to Hold Your Hand* and *Wild Thing* all use these three chords in very different ways. In order to see where the roots of the three chord change originated, it is necessary to understand the standard twelve bar blues.

The Blues

An example of a typical blues pattern is the *twelve bar blues*. The best way to establish a measurement or division of beat is to count out loud 1, 2, 3, 4, 1, 2, 3, 4, 1, 2, 3, 4. For the sake of understanding the concept of this example, the count can take place at any speed. The twelve bar blues has twelve sets of four counts. The chord changes are played in relation to the four count sets in the following sequence.

Diagram 7   The twelve bar blues

1	2	3	4	5	6	7	8
E	E	E	E	A	A	E	E
1 2 3 4	1 2 3 4	1 2 3 4	1 2 3 4	1 2 3 4	1 2 3 4	1 2 3 4	1 2 3 4

9	10	11	12
B	A	E	B
1 2 3 4	1 2 3 4	1 2 3 4	1 2 3 4

Here is an alternative arrangement of the above example.

Diagram 8   Twelve bar blues variation

1	2	3	4	5	6	7	8
E	A	E	E	A	A	E	E
1 2 3 4	1 2 3 4	1 2 3 4	1 2 3 4	1 2 3 4	1 2 3 4	1 2 3 4	1 2 3 4

9	10	11	12
B	B	E	E
1 2 3 4	1 2 3 4	1 2 3 4	1 2 3 4

In order to really experience this structure, count out loud and tap your foot to the count and play the chords to the changes. You don't have to make music. All that is necessary to understand the idea is to strum the designated chord once on the count of one.

Chuck Berry used the twelve bar structure when he wrote *Johnny be Good*. The twelve bar blues example lies at the foundation of chord changes in rock music.

The *eight bar blues* uses the same four count bars found in the twelve bar blues but returns to the first after only eight bars. The following example shows the chord changes in the song *Bring it on Home*. Because of the chord changes within the four count bar, it is necessary to show the chord used with each count of the eight bars.

Diagram 9   The eight bar blues

1	2	3	4	5	6	7	8
E E E E	B B B B	E E E E	A A A A	E E E E	B B B B	E E A A	E E B B
1 2 3 4	1 2 3 4	1 2 3 4	1 2 3 4	1 2 3 4	1 2 3 4	1 2 3 4	1 2 3 4

Relative Chords

In order to study the complete chord network which produces the ingredients of song structure, it is necessary to understand the function of relative chords. The three basic chords in rock music form a pattern used to establish relative chord patterns which are also common to a given key.

Relative Minor Chords

Each major chord has a relative minor chord. The relative minor chord takes its position *three frets below* the major chord in the *form of a minor*. For instance, the relative minor to the D major chord is the B minor chord. Each of the three major chords which are common to the blues song structure has its own relative minor chord. The three relative minor chords to the basic blues chords in the key of A are graphically shown below.

Diagram 10   Basic and relative minor chords–Key of A

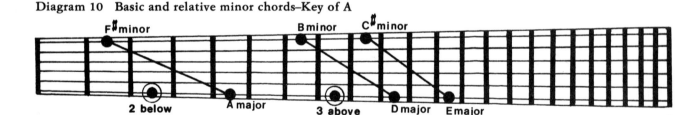

In addition to the six chords we have already studied, there are also *two other common chords* which take their position in relation to the root/chord.

Two Frets Below

This chord takes is position two frets below the root chord in the form of a major chord. In the key of E, a D major chord would be indicated.

Three Frets Above

The last chord we will consider takes its place three frets above the root chord in the form of a major chord. In the key of E, a G major would be the indicated chord.

Songwriting

The eight common chords described above are generally used to construct popular music. When a songwriter sits down to work, it is with these chord combinations that he labors. We have taken a look at how to establish which chords are common to a given key, but it is also important to understand how chords work with each other to create the fabric of the music. If the concept of relative chords is new to you, page through a popular songbook and work out the chord changes to a few songs. Take note of how the three basic chords are used with relative chords to form the flow of the music.

Pick out a familiar song which uses five or six chords. Carefully study the component chords noting the key which is being used. Then identify which of the eight common chords correspond with each chord in the song. Make notes on the sequence of the chords especially which ones begin and end the verse and bridge.

Recorded music is more difficult to work with but knowing how to analyze the chords to a song can be of great value particularly if you are in a band. Trying to find the key of a song can often be a jig-saw puzzle until you have enough facts to fit it all together. For instance, if a song starts with a rhythm created by the A minor and the F major chord you may have to wait until the bridge of the song uses the G chord to realize that the song is being played in the key of C. The three basic chords to the key of C are C, F and G. A minor is the relative minor to C major.

Now let's turn our attention to a few of the songwriting techniques that we will find when we analyze rock music. When we trace the roots of rock influence, the blues structure is found to be fundamental. The twelve and eight bar blues structure seem simple enough upon first encounter, but if you account for forty years of development by millions of musicians in America and the world, what we have is a complex architecture using simple elements. The blues are only a skeleton from which chord changes and relationships are incorporated into the structure of new songs. The most elementary of all two chord blues relationships is between the root chord and the second basic chord. The song *Day Tripper*, recorded by the Beatles, uses the first eight bars of the twelve bar blues to carry the song's riff through the standard two chord changes. After this point, the song leaves the blues structure and employs a chord sequence using all three relative minor chords before it ends on the third basic major chord.

The *turnaround* is a songwriting technique that employs basic and relative chords in short combinations to form a musical wheel that smoothly returns to its starting point to turn over again and again. The most common form of the turnaround uses the three basic chords and the relative minor to the first basic. In the key of C, play the four chords in this sequence with four equal counts to each chord: C, A minor, F, G7.

The next example is a chord sequence that builds on the turnaround principle. Although the entire sequence can be considered a unit, it contains two turnarounds in the key of E, the first one ending on a relative minor and the second one ending on the third basic major chord.

E	C#m	A	F#m	E	C#m	A	B
1 2 3 4	1 2 3 4	1 2 3 4	1 2 3 4	1 2 3 4	1 2 3 4	1 2 3 4	1 2 3 4

The best way to learn how rock music uses chord change is to listen closely to music with the intention of identifying the elements or techniques being used. Listen closely for blues influence, turnarounds, extended bridges, introductions, and endings. Hard rockers are usually borrowing directly from the twelve bar blues and often use a song bridge of the two major relative chords positioned two frets below and three frets above the root. The repeated riff motif is also very common in rock songs. The song *Jumping Jack Flash*, written by Keith Richard and Mick Jagger, pounds out an eight count riff which works directly with the root chord. The riff repeats four times before the turnaround bridge which contains the two relative major chords.

Melodic songs are more likely to use a flowing chord arrangement which employs a verse and chorus containing turnarounds and relative minor chords.

Diagram 11   Common chord chart

KEY	E	A	D	G	B
CHORD					
1st Basic root or tonic	E	A	D	G	B
2nd Basic five frets above root	A	D	G	C	E
3rd Basic seven frets above root	B	E	A	D	F#
Relative minor to 1st Basic	C# minor	F# minor	B minor	E minor	G# minor
Relative minor to 2nd Basic	F# minor	B minor	E minor	A minor	C# minor
Relative minor to 3rd Basic	G# minor	C# minor	F# minor	B minor	D# minor
Relative 2 frets below root	D	G	C	F	A
Relative 3 frets above root	G	C	F	A#	D

28

THE SIX LINE STAFF

Invention of the line staff is ascribed to Guido Arezzo (995-1050) who recommended the use of three or four lines. Five line staffs were used as early as 1200. In the 16th century, staffs with up to eight lines were employed for keyboard music.

The Heavy Guitar Bible uses a six line staff representing the six strings of the guitar. Numbers and letters are used on the staff to show the exact sequence in which a series of notes follow each other, the fret and string on which each note is to be played, and the finger of the left hand that is used for fretting each note.

Transcription 0

- The lines of the staff represent the six strings of the guitar the way they would appear if the guitar were on your lap with the body of the guitar on your right leg.
- The bottom line represents the low E string and each ascending line represents the next higher string.
- A number, as it appears on a given line (string), represents the fret on which the note is to be played.
- A letter appearing below the bottom line under each number indicates the finger of the left hand to be used in fretting the note (I-index, M-middle, R-ring, P-pinky, O-played open).

Throughout the book the term transcription is used to indicate a six line staff. Each transcription is numbered and labeled for key. The transcription above illustrates the sequence of notes that results when an E major chord is strummed from the low E string to the high E string.

Four symbols are used to indicate specific techniques. The symbol appears above or between the notes involved. Explanations of the various techniques are given as they are introduced.

Symbol	Technique
U	Slide Up
∩	Slide Down
B	Bend
P	Pull

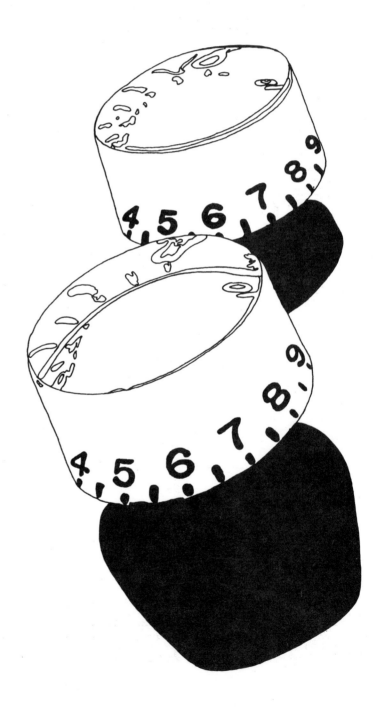

4
THE BLUES

A musical scale is a selected series of notes from the twelve note octave. Different scales can vary in both the *number* and *choice* of notes. The most elementary scale is the *chromatic* which contains every note in the twelve note octave. A *diatonic* scale contains seven degrees and usually refers to the major scale. This chapter introduces a *pentatonic* scale which is composed of five notes. For more information on scales refer to *Scale Expo* and *Building* (Chapters 11 and 12).

The most important musical scale to the rock guitarist is the *blues scale*. The blues scale is composed of five notes and is therefore a pentatonic scale. In the key of E these five notes are E, G, A, B & D. For the rest of the book the word *blues* will be used interchangably with the term *blues scale*.

This diagram shows the notes of the blues scale on the low E string from the open E note to the octave at the twelfth fret. Above the twelfth fret the pattern repeats itself.

Diagram 12   Blues scale on low E string–Key of E

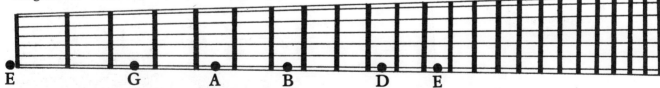

E   G   A   B   D   E

In the same way that the twelve notes of the octave repeat themselves as they climb up the fretboard, the five notes that are particular to the blues scale cut a definite pattern on the fretboard. Here is the all-important blues scale as it appears on all six strings in the key of E.

Diagram 13   Blues scale–Key of E

G   A   B   D   E   G   B

31

The Root Note Fret

The notes in the above pattern form a basic frame of reference for the rock guitarist. The blues scale is a cookie cutter pattern that repeats itself *every twelve frets*. The fret on which the *letter name of the key* appears on the low E string is known as the *root note fret*. The root note fret is unique because it is the only fret in the *twelve fret repeating pattern* that contains notes from the blues pattern on *all six strings across the fret*. This feature of the root note fret is used to visually seat the pattern in any key for its use all over the fretboard. Because the fretboard is twenty two frets long, there will always be two root note frets for any given key, which will appear twelve frets apart.

In the above example for the key of E, the first root note fret appears across the six open strings at the bottom of the fretboard. The second is positioned one octave above at the twelfth fret. Please note the six black dots straight across this fret. The total pattern of any musical scale repeats itself every octave the same way as the single notes on any string.

The notes wait in their pattern like words in a dictionary, to be used in a creative sequence. This can vary from a single note riff by Chuck Berry through the top speed scale climbing of Alvin Lee, to the use of the scale as a fluid vehicle by Hendrix or Page.

Boxes

In order to have a basic understanding of the positions of the notes in the blues scale, it is necessary to become familiar with the way rock guitarists pass through the notes of the scale as they unfold on the fretboard. In the Key of E, the blues can be divided into a number of patterns where the notes form a climb up the scale *in the same sequence* that they progress up the low E string from the bottom. That sequence again is: E, G, A, B, D.

Diagram 14   Blues scale with common boxes–Key of E

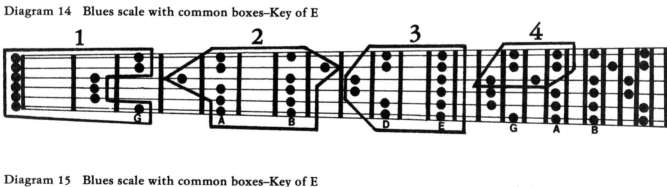

Diagram 15   Blues scale with common boxes–Key of E

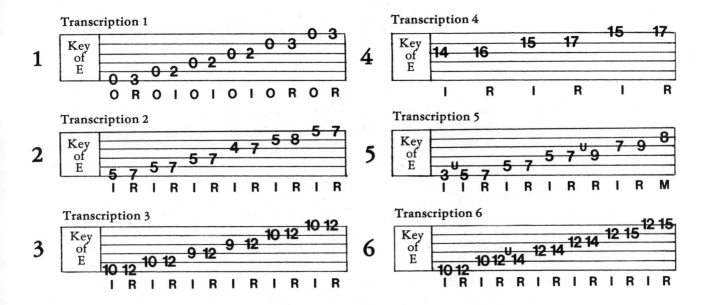

Transcription 1

1

Key of E

									0 3
						0 2	0 3	
				0 2	0 2			
		0 2						
0 3	0 2							

O R O I O I O I O R O R

Transcription 4

4

Key of E

					15	17
			15	17		
14	16					

I R I R I R

Transcription 2

2

Key of E

							5 7
				5 8		
			4 7			
	5 7	5 7				
5 7						

I R I R I R I R I R I R

Transcription 5

5

Key of E

							8
					7 9	
			5 7	⌣9		
		5 7				
3 ⌣5 7						

I I R I R I R R I R M

Transcription 3

3

Key of E

						10 12
				10 12		
		9 12	9 12			
	10 12					
10 12						

I R I R I R I R I R I R

Transcription 6

6

Key of E

							12 15
					12 15	
				12 14		
		10 12 ⌣14	12 14			
10 12						

I R I R R I R I R I R I R

The six boxes from the above example are all subsets from the complete twelve-fret scale pattern. Box 1 is the most frequently used and easily recognized reference point for lead guitar work. The bottom of the box is formed by the six open strings across the root note fret, while the upper part is composed of easily fingered notes positioned two and three frets above the root note fret.

Together, boxes 1, 2 and 3 form a neat package which play every single note from the top, middle and bottom of the twelve fret repeating blues pattern. Note how the upper part of box 3 is formed by the root note fret at the twelfth fret —the same notes which form the bottom of box one.

Boxes 4, 5 and 6 combine parts of boxes 1, 2 and 3 to explore the middle ground between the first three boxes. Box 4 is a unit composed of the top of box 1 and the bottom of box 2 using the first three strings. Box 5 opens up box 2 from the top and the bottom. Box 6 is box 1 played at the octave (twelfth fret), with two notes on the tenth fret borrowed from box 3.

It is far more important to become *familiar* with the right notes in practice than it is to memorize the boxes from the above example. These boxes are obviously just a few of the hundreds of ways in which the scale pattern can be divided. The box system, by its nature, is a division of the entire scale. The boxes should not be seen as barriers. They are tools used to help envision the territory presented by the entire pattern. The box system is of little value when you become familiar with chord changes and you want to play lead riffs off the chord. When the guitarist has evolved to this point, he looks at the chord, whatever position, and tries to envision which part of the blues pattern immediately surrounds the chord. This is why memorizing the total picture of the scale pattern is important.

The example below transcends the box system and runs the whole board in just the blues scale.

Diagram 16   Blues scale with extended box–Key of E

Transcription 7

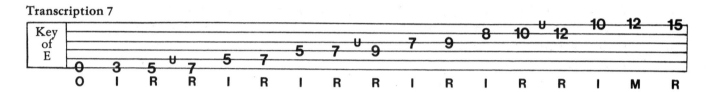

There are several different fingering possibilities for any riff that moves up or down the board in a continuum. If you paid close attention to the transcription above, you noted the symbol for the slide up (u) appears between two notes played by the *ring finger* (see sliding in appendix). The same series of notes is transcribed below changing the slide to the *index finger*. Subtle variations in fingering technique can make all the difference in the world. Use whichever method you find most comfortable.

Transcription 8

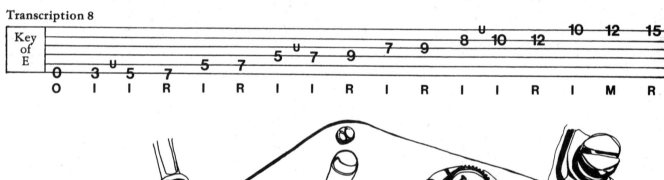

TRANSPOSING

Any musical chord, scale or riff is universal and can be played in any key. The same basic principles that are used to form bar chords at different frets can also be used to transpose musical scales. The word transpose can be defined as *adjusting for key*.

The notes on the low E string are the basic reference points for transposing. The *letter name of the key* is matched with the *same letter name note* on the low E string. The fret at which this note appears will be the *root note fret* for that key.

The cookie cutter pattern of the blues scale moves up and down the fretboard with a *root note fret adjustment* made for a particular key. The root note fret is unique because it is the only fret in the twelve fret repeating pattern that contains notes from the blues pattern on *all six strings across the fret*. This feature of the root note fret is used to visually seat the pattern for its use all over the fretboard. Because the fretboard is twenty-two frets long there will always be *two* root note frets which appear twelve frets apart.

The examples below show the blues scale in the key of E, A and D. The root note frets in the key of E appear at the twelfth fret and across the open strings. In the key of A the root note frets are the fifth and the seventeenth. In the key of D, the tenth and the twenty-second fret contain the root note.

Diagram 17   Blues scale with root note frets boxed–Key of E

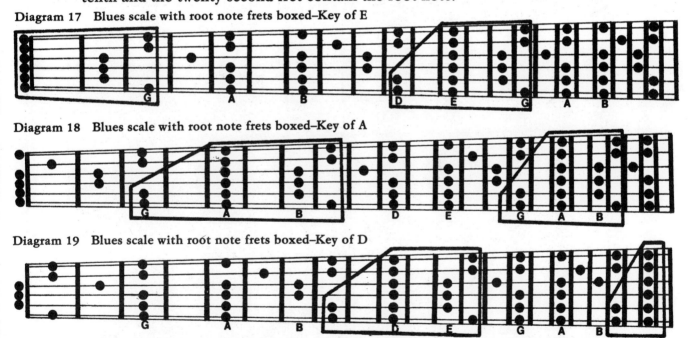

Diagram 18   Blues scale with root note frets boxed–Key of A

Diagram 19   Blues scale with root note frets boxed–Key of D

The notes *on and around the root note fret* have been outlined in order to illustrate the different positions of the root note fret in different keys. Notice that the two notes played on the fifth and sixth string, two frets *below* the root note fret, do not appear in the key of E where the root note fret is considered the open strings, but at the octave (twelfth fret) the pattern is complete.

Because the root note fret appears on a different fret in each key, a study should be made of the positioning characteristics of the blues pattern in each key. Because a great deal of rock guitar is played in the keys of A and E, these two keys will be used for examples in this book.

35

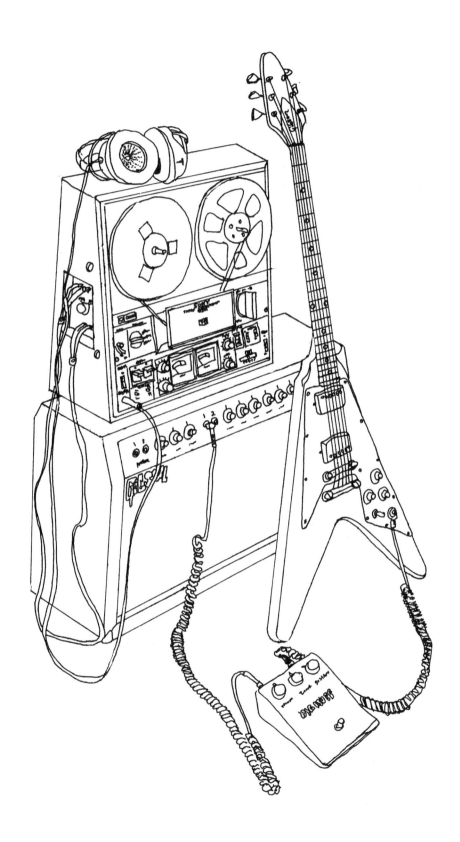

5
BLUES
APPROACHES

p to this point the book has presented facts on the formation of scales and other basic information. Most of the attention has been focused on where the right notes are located. We will now set our sights on the *use* of the blues scale from the viewpoint of the rock guitarist.

This chapter presents a series of eight *conceptual approaches* to the *entire blues scale*. Different approaches have been lifted from the music of rock guitarists and will be examined separately. Each approach is a musical framework that enables the guitarist to become familiar with the notes of the scale using a repeating pattern as a basic unit. The various approaches help the guitarist to *see* the notes in their stationary patterns being used to form fluid, creative ideas.

The purpose of this chapter is to expose the blues scale as a variable unit which can be approached in any number of ways. Each different approach passes through the blues scale using *every note of this scale* in its structure.

This most popular and accessible part of the blues is the series of notes on and around the root note fret. This fret is unique because it is the only fret of the twelve fret repeating pattern that contains a note from the blues *on each string*. This positioning will be used as the basic reference point for most of the approaches.

The word *ascending* means playing upward through the scale while the term *descending* means the opposite. The approaches in this book use both techniques but only one is used for each approach. Be aware that any approach can be played using the ascending or descending method.

Approach One

The first approach is given in two different positions both in the key of A. The five note scale has been divided into triplets composed of two notes. Concentrate on the triplet as a unit by counting one, two, three...one, two, three. If this is the first time that you have transcribed the six line staff notation into real guitar work, give yourself a few minutes to simply work it out. Don't give up. Struggle with the book and then put the book away, playing the riff for your own enjoyment.

Diagram 20 Blues scale–Key of A

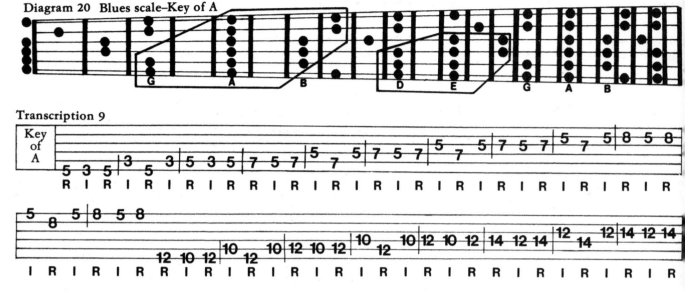

Transcription 9

Transcription 10

All of the approaches should be practiced until they become second nature and very little concentration is needed to perform them. Once you get the feel of performing the above triplet, it can be used anywhere on the fretboard in the universal blues pattern. To explore this possibility, the next example uses the same triplet from the above example but plays it using an expanded arrangement.

Approach Two

The next approach is an interesting arrangement which uses two sets of two notes. Practice this series of two notes until you can play them fast and easy to create a smooth flowing effect. The same two positions in the key of A that were used for Approach One is used here.

Transcription 11

When playing Approach Two, use the index and ring finger to fret two strings at the same time where it is possible. The technique is essentially a two finger bar that increases playing speed while two strings are allowed to sound at the same time. Here is an illustration of this technique.

Hand Illustration 5
Index Finger barring first and second string

Hand Illustration 6
Ring Finger barring second and third string

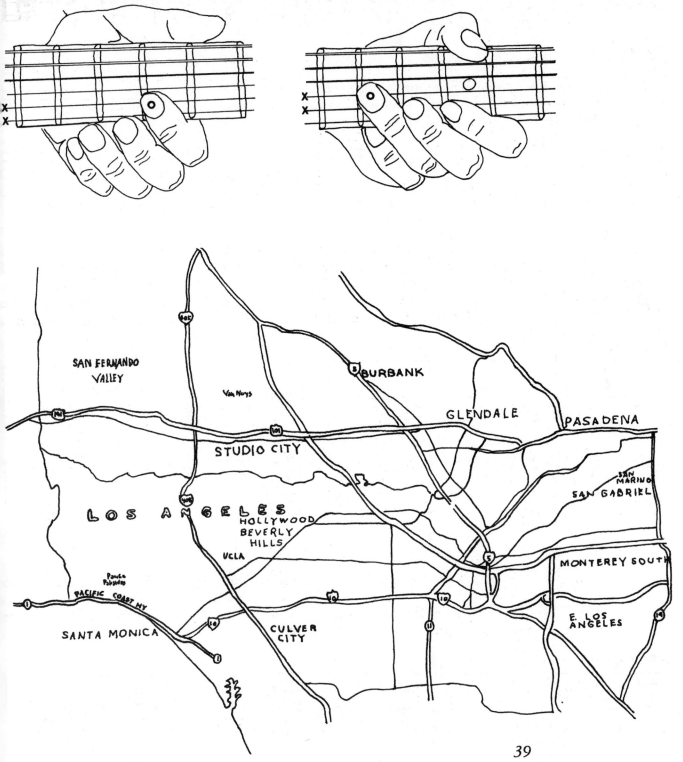

Approach Three

This approach uses a four note repeating riff as a vehicle. The four note series used is more of a true guitar riff than the series of notes that compose the other blues approaches.

Transcription 12

Approaches four through eight are studies in three, four, five and six note series that progressively descend through the blues scale. Each set of notes follows in direct sequence the course of the five note scale. The starting note of any given set is one note *lower* on the scale than the previous set. Examples are given in the key of E at the open root note fret (the six open strings).

Diagram 21   Blues scale–Key of E

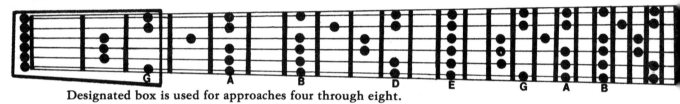

Designated box is used for approaches four through eight.

Approach Four

Transcription 13

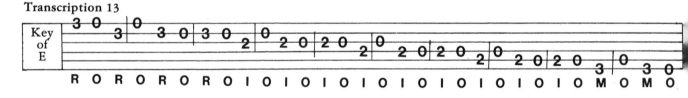

Approach Five

Transcription 14

Approach Six

Transcription 15

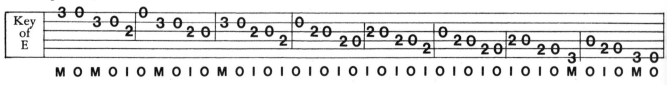

40

Approach Seven

M O M O I O O M O I O I M O I O I O O I O I O I I O I O I O O I O I O M I O I O M O

Approach Eight

Approach Eight uses a double triplet in its construction. The three note series from Approach Four is used with a second complimentary triplet played with each original triplet.

Transcription 17

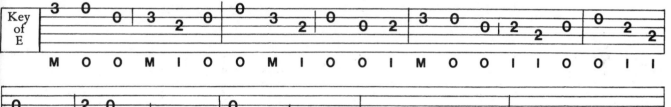

M O O M I O O M I O O I M O O I I O O I I

O O I I O O I I O O I I O O I I O O I M O O I M O O M

Depending upon how well you play the guitar, you have gone through the pages of this book at your own speed, passing over those things with which you are already familiar. An initial working knowledge is all that is necessary for the understanding of bar chords and octave structure as explained in the opening chapters. However this is not so for the various blues approaches.

The first time that you sit down with a tuned guitar and the transcriptions of the above approaches, it may take you three or four minutes to get through each exercise. Do not make the mistake of letting *basic understanding* take the place of becoming *truly familiar* with the different approaches. Just to understand how the patterns work is *not enough!* You have to impress your mind with these patterns and this can only be done by repeating them over and over and over, up and down. Conscious practice of these blues approaches is *the way* to become familiar with the fretboard. The benefit of this type of practice will take place when you improvise. You will find that you have greater dexterity, confidence and an improved musical vocabulary. The systems of the different approaches will percolate into your usual style of playing.

Practice running the blues up and down using the various approaches with the attitude that you are practicing with the instrument and not making music. Run the scale up and down until it sounds hypnotic and mathematic. This is the type of practice that classical piano players always receive early in their training. So do yourself a favor and take the time to practice.

Services held at midnight, Friday and Saturday.

6
THE RELATIVE

The next step toward complete understanding of heavy rock guitar is the concept of the *relative scale*. The relative scale is a selection of notes from the twelve note octave, but differs from the blues scale because it is a different series of notes.

The relative scale is a five note scale which is *IDENTICAL TO THE BLUES SCALE IN EVERY WAY WITH THE EXCEPTION OF ITS POSITION*. The pattern of the relative scale takes its place on the fretboard exactly *THREE FRETS BELOW THE BLUES SCALE PATTERN*.

Because the relative scale is located three frets below the blues and has the same pattern, the relative scale in the key of E is the same as the blues in the key of C♯. The relative scale in the key of A is the same as the blues in the key of F♯.

The particular sound of the relative scale works on the same principle as the relative minor chords discussed in the section *relative chords* (chapter three). Relative scales have a very interesting sound which is subtle and smooth when compared to the blues. The blues scale is up front and most hard riffs are played strictly in the blues. The relative scale has an indescribable sound that is mathematically relative to the blues. It is often referred to as the country scale because of its

Diagram 22   Blues scale – Key of E

Diagram 23   Relative scale–Key of E

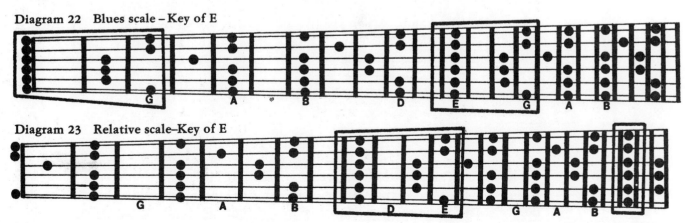

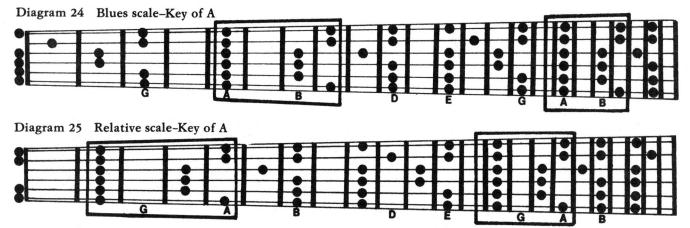

Diagram 24   Blues scale–Key of A

G   A   B   D   E   G   A   B

Diagram 25   Relative scale–Key of A

G   A   B   D   E   G   A   B

use in country and blue grass music. The melody line to many rock songs works itself out directly in the relative scale. After becoming familiar with both scales you can easily distinguish which scale a guitarist is using.

The relative scale adds a whole new dimension to the possibilities of playing lead guitar. Because it is identical to the blues scale in its nature (same pattern and same number of notes) the relative scale can be studied in the same way as the blues scale. This includes the breakdown into boxes from transcriptions 1 through 6, and the systems introduced in Chapter 5 – *Blues Approaches*.

Here is an exercise in the Key of A to become familiar with the difference in the sound and position of the two scales. Play an A major chord and create a rhythm or simply strum it and let the strings ring. Now play these notes in the blues scale.

Transcription 18

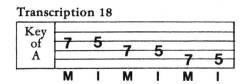

| Key of A | 7 5   7 5   7 5 |

M   I   M   I   M   I

Strum the chord again and then play this riff. It is the same riff as the one above except it takes its position in the relative scale.

Transcription 19

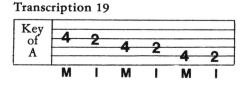

| Key of A | 4 2   4 2   4 2 |

M   I   M   I   M   I

Both the blues and relative are five note scales taken from the twelve notes of the octave. *IMPORTANT FACT: Two of the five notes* in each scale are *common to both scales*. To the five note blues scale, therefore, it is only necessary to add three notes to also embrace the relative scale. This leads to a very important concept concerning the use of both scales.

The Two Scale Relationship

The blues scale is a definite pattern, a recognizable unit that covers the entire fretboard. The goal of the serious guitarist is to envision the pattern anywhere on the fretboard so he can confidently play the right notes. If the guitarist is familiar

44

enough with the blues pattern to *see* it on the fretboard, to play in the relative scale he *sees* the same pattern three frets below.

The following diagram shows both the blues and the relative scales superimposed on the fretboard. The blues scale is shown in *black dots* and the relative is shown in *circles*. Notes with both circles and dots are those that are *common to both scales*.

Diagram 26   Blues and relative scales superimposed–Key of E

Diagram 27   Blues and relative scales superimposed–Key of A

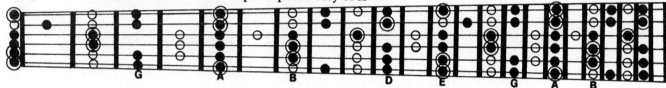

Practically all rock guitar leads are based on the relationship between these two scales. The diagrams above appear overwhelming in their complexity, but they are much easier to understand when either of the two scales are envisioned separately.

The rock guitarist approaches the relationship between the blues and the relative scale using one of these four techniques:

● Technique A – The blues scale is used exclusively.
● Technique B – The relative scale is used exclusively.
● Technique C – The three notes of the relative scale that are *note common* to both
scales are used as fillers or additions to riffs that are based in the
blues scale.
● Technique D – The three notes of the blues scale that are *not common* to both
scales are used as fillers or additions to riffs that are based in the
relative scale.

In order to simplify the diagrams with both scales superimposed, the next two diagrams present a blueprint for technique C. The full blues scale is diagrammed in *black dots* with the additional notes provided by the relative scale represented by *circles*.

Diagram 28   Blues scale with filler notes from relative–Key of E

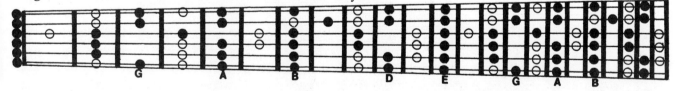

Diagram 29   Blues scale with filler notes from relative–Key of A

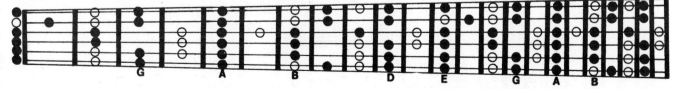

The following two diagrams present a blueprint for technique D. The complete relative scale is diagrammed in *black dots* with the additional notes provided by the blues scale represented by *circles*.

Diagram 30   Relative scale with filler notes from blues–Key of E

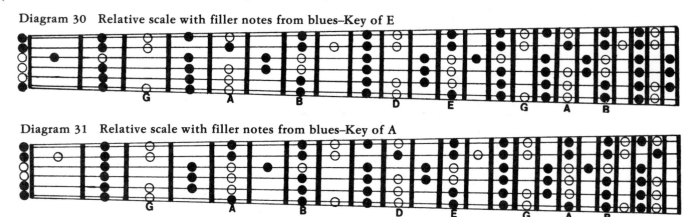

Diagram 31   Relative scale with filler notes from blues–Key of A

When the lead guitar breaks to the great hard rock songs are analyzed, all four techniques (A,B,C and D) are found to be freely interchanged, often *in the same guitar break*. The change from one technique to the next may take place very quickly. The artist may be playing very fast using only riffs taken from the blues scale. When the feeling is right, he may play just one or two riffs, just a few seconds of music, using the relative scale. He may then choose to play riffs that are based in the blues but borrow selected notes from the relative. Chapter 11, *Scale Expo*, explores complete scales which can be formed from the combination of both of the basic five note scales.

Here is an example of technique C. It uses notes from both scales in its structure but is based on the root note fret for the blues scale.

Transcription 20

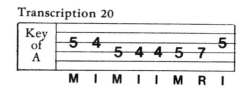

The following is a lead guitar break transcribed in the key of A. Note how the lead switches back and forth between both scales. The relationship between the scales is shown by a letter designating which technique (A,B or C) is being used.

Transcription 21

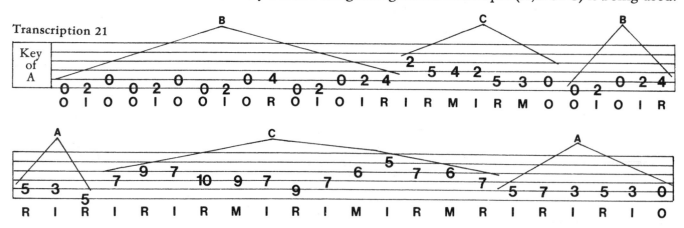

46

7
MIXED APPROACHES

hapter five gave eight workable approaches that used only the notes of the blues scale. The previous chapter introduced another five note scale, the relative, and also explained the possibilities for combining the two scales.

This chapter will present several more approaches that are based in the blues scale, but in their construction use the three additional notes provided by the relative scale (two notes are common to each scale).

Here is a short study to become familiar with where the three extra relative notes appear around the *blues root note fret*. The diagram below illustrates the notes on and around the root note fret in the key of A.

Diagram 32   Blues scale root note fret–Key of A

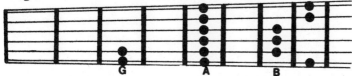

Transcription 22

The three additional notes of the relative scale appear in three clusters around the notes in the above diagram of the blues scale. The next diagram shows the position of these three clusters.

Diagram 33   Blues scale with relative note clusters–Key of A

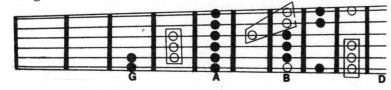

Transcription 23

The two clusters that appear on the lower strings are composed of identical notes from the same octave but are shown in different positions. Note that the

above diagram is only a six fret segment of the complete fretboard network shown in diagram 29.

The *mixed approaches* take the notes that appear in the clusters and combine them with riffs that are based in the blues scale. Many of the *blues approaches* were designed as finger exercises as well as being a vehicle to instruct. The *mixed approaches* are closer to actual guitar riffs because they represent a recognizable musical statement. The *mixed approaches* use only one of the three relative notes in each "unit pattern." All of the mixed approaches have three or less riffs per octave.

Several of the approaches use double triplets as a vehicle that divide each octave into two distinct riffs. All of the unit patterns that compose the approaches in this chapter should be studied as *individual riffs* as well as fluid vehicles for moving through the octaves.

Triplets

One of the essential divisions given to the octave by blues guitarists is the triplet. This section presents the basic single triplet and then the double triplet.

The single triplets are based entirely in the blues scale. The most popular and convenient way to divide the octave with single triplets is with two sets of triplets (six notes) which use the five notes of the blues scale plus the root note one octave below the starting note. The triplets take place between the open high E string and the open low E string. This is a measurement of exactly two octaves with the first octave ending on the second fret of the fourth string (D string). Each octave is divided into two triplets, one starting with an E note and the other with an A note. Since we have two octaves in the example, there will be four triplets.

Diagram 34   Blues scale–Key of E

Transcription 24

Mixed Approach One – The Double Triplet

As the basics of musical structure became familiar to the pioneers of rock guitar technique, they pushed their lead guitar work into increasingly complex patterns. To construct the more complex double triplet, the triplet series from the above example is broken down with an additional relative triplet being added to each existing triplet. The first example is transcribed in the key of A (root note fret is fifth fret). After going through the transcription a few times, to see how these notes fit into the overall pattern, find the location of the relative notes in diagram 33.

Transcription 25

48

The double triplet is a unique vehicle for expression. It is a dynamic riff that was lifted from a song by Jimmy Page called *Good Times/Bad Times*, the first song on the first side of Led Zeppelin's first album.

Extended Double Triplet

The following example shows how the double triplet can be played as a continuous flowing run that traverses the fretboard. A review diagram of the blues scale and a diagram of the notes used in the transcription are given below.

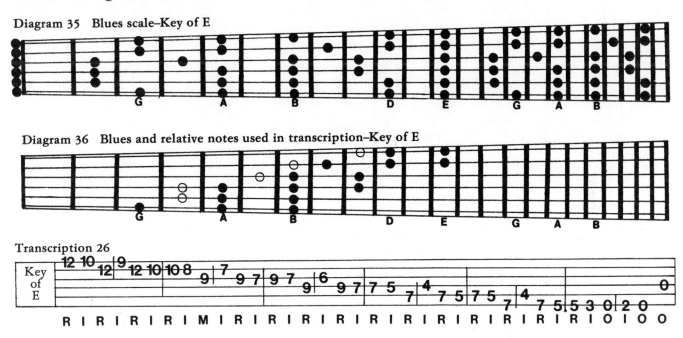

Diagram 35   Blues scale–Key of E

Diagram 36   Blues and relative notes used in transcription–Key of E

Transcription 26

Mixed Approach Two

This approach uses *two sets* of *four notes*. The second set contains a relative note.

Transcription 27

Here is the basic series of notes from Mixed Approach Two played in three consecutive octaves.

Transcription 28

Mixed Approach Three

This is a double triplet that has been transcribed in both the keys of A and E. This was done to show how the same riff can be executed in two different keys. It also shows the different position possibilities of each root note fret.

Transcription 29

Transcription 30

Mixed Approach Four

This is a double triplet similar in structure to Mixed Approach One.

Transcription 31

Mixed Approach Five

This is a unique triplet that appears twice in each octave. It shows a truly composite riff which freely uses notes from other scales.

Transcription 32

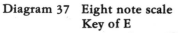

Mixed Approach Six

Approach Six uses the five notes of the Blues and the three added notes from the relative scale as an eight note scale. This scale is the key to playing lead guitar. This special scale has been transcribed in the keys of A and E.

Diagram 37   Eight note scale
Key of E

Transcription 33

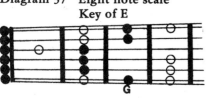
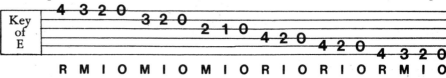

50

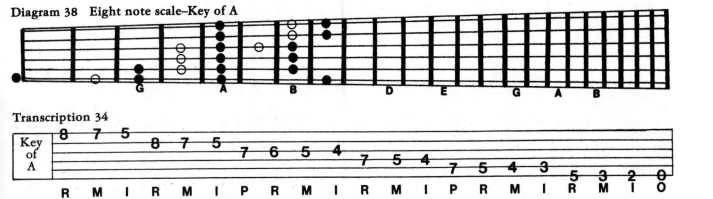

Diagram 38   Eight note scale–Key of A

Transcription 34

Key of A

| 8 | 7 | 5 | | | | | | | | | | | | | | | | | | | |

R M I R M I P R M I R M I P R M I R M I O

A Note on the Approaches

When you practice the approaches, both the *blues* and the *mixed*, concentrate on an even, systematic timing as each set of notes is played. The approaches using the double and single triplet in their design are constantly used in heavy rock improvising. When guitarists play live sets and have to improvise for ten or fifteen minutes, you will hear them fall back on a *patterned approach* to the basic scales. The approaches in this book were taken directly from the music of the greatest guitarists in rock. If the approaches are played regularly they will start the wheels turning towards developing your own fluid, professional style.

Your Practice Time

There is a lot to consider when you want to design a good way to practice the guitar. It is always hard to find enough time. In the appendix of the book, you will find a section called *Blues Review* which will take you through the master pattern a few new ways. Here is a suggested outline that you should include in your practice.

- A study of the blues scale pattern using transcriptions 1 through 7. Finger the pattern both ascending and descending in the key of E and A.
- Do the same study with the relative scale in the keys of E and A.
- Go over the approaches one by one, both blues and mixed.

When the scales and the approaches are systematically practiced you will become familiar with all eight notes just by their sound. You will transcend the diagrams as you absorb the ideas that they offer. The approaches are not a guitar style in themselves, although they will form a strong base for improvising. Their most important role is to allow you to become visually familiar with the patterns of the two scales and to influence your mind in such a way that you will be able to control the fretboard and use the right notes off the top of your head.

THE GOLDEN RULE

Here it is pure and simple. The notes on and around the Root Note Fret.

Key of A

G   A   B   D   E

GET IT RIGHT

8
HEAVY RIFFS

ock guitar has definite roots. Most of the basic riff techniques can be traced back directly to the acoustic styles of the old blues masters. Electric guitar artists, using volume and sustain, use these early guitar styles to create their own category of riffs that are used almost exclusively in blues and rock music.

Because the majority of the artists who had influence on the early blues scene were self taught, their riffs were created just for the sound that they made, using the position where they could be most easily played. The fundamental elements of blues guitar structure are the notes of the *Golden Rule* and the overlapping patterns of the E major and A major chords on the root note fret. The most popular position for heavy riffs is on and around the root note fret on the first, second and third strings.

Because this selection of notes spans the twelve note octave(C note to another C note), any riff can be performed within its boundaries.

Before we look at the riffs, we will study the technique needed to perform them. The two techniques that make the distinct difference in the heavy riffs are the bend and the pull. The pull is discussed later in this chapter. There are also several techniques, such as vibrato, that can make a great difference in total sound and these more subtle fingering and plucking techniques are discussed in the appendix.

Diagram 39   Blues scale root note fret–Key of A

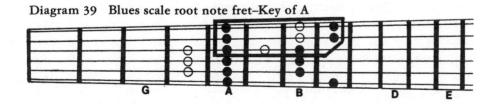

Bending

To bend a note, fret and pluck as usual, then push the string across the fretboard keeping it firmly fretted under the finger. This action results in raising the pitch of the original fretted note that was plucked. Bent notes are usually used in a riff with several other notes, but can be used to make a single note riff.

The most popular position for bent string riffs is on and immediately above the root note fret on the first three strings shown in the above diagram. When this position is used the index finger acts as a bar across the first two strings on the root note fret.

In the two hand illustrations below, notice how the index finger acts as a bar and how the ring finger bends the third string.

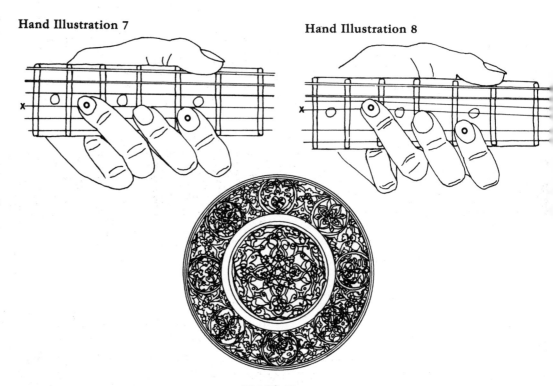

Hand Illustration 7

Hand Illustration 8

Riff One

Here is what you have been waiting for. Each riff is shown in the key of A and has a transcription of the notes used in the riff, a hand illustration and a diagram of other places where the riff can be performed.

This example uses the most frequently bent note in rock music. Depending on personal preference, this note can be bent from the second or third fret above the root note fret on the third string. The third fret is used in this example. Whichever you decide to use, bend the note until it sounds the note normally fretted on the fourth fret above the root note fret. Remember, the index finger acts as a bar across the root note fret on the first two strings.

Where it is necessary, the hand illustrations in this book have a small number on the fretboard which indicates the root note fret position. In the following diagrams, a circle represents the note being bent.

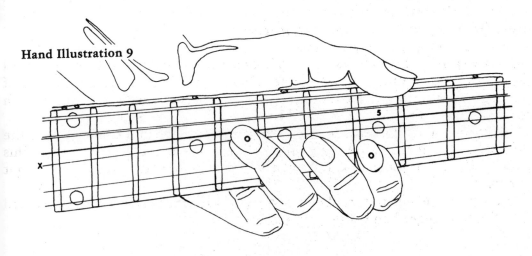

Hand Illustration 9

Diagram 40   Note used in transcription – Key of A

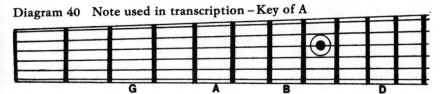

G   A   B   D

Transcription 35

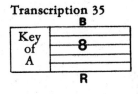

Diagram 41   Blues scale other positions–Key of A

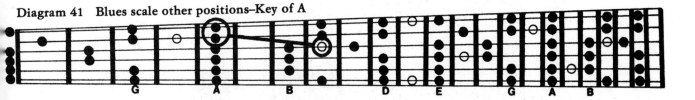

G   A   B   D   E   G   A   B

Riff Two

This riff uses the single bent note from riff one in combination with the note played on the second string by the index finger. The two notes that compose this bent note riff can be plucked and bent separately sounding the second note afterward, or with both notes being sounded simultaneously with a single picking movement. In the following transcriptions, the second method will be noted by the placing of two numbers (notes) directly over each other.

The secret to this riff is bending the first note until it sounds the same note as the second note being held by the index finger. Bend it smooth and easy until they are the same. The hand illustration for riff one is also used for riff two and three.

Diagram 42   Notes used in transcription–Key of A

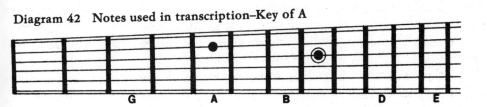

G   A   B   D   E

Transcription 36

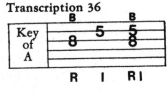

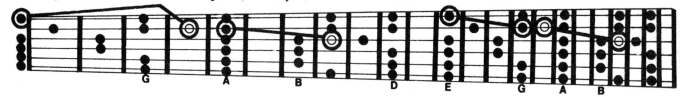

Diagram 43   Blues scale other positions–Key of A

Riff Three

This is a three note riff which is the same as riff one except it uses the first string in its construction. Riff one, two and three are practically the same, however, together they offer an introduction to the most fundamental lead guitar position from which other riffs are built. Note the three different combinations of notes in the transcription.

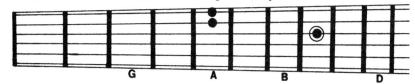

Diagram 44   Notes used in transcription–Key of A

Transcription 37

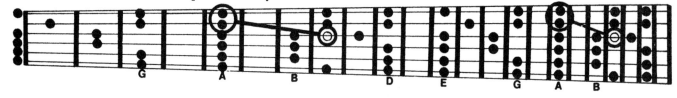

Diagram 45   Blues scale other positions–Key of A

Riff Four

This riff bends the third string with the middle finger and frets the second string with the ring finger. Both strings are played three frets above the root note fret.

Hand Illustration 10

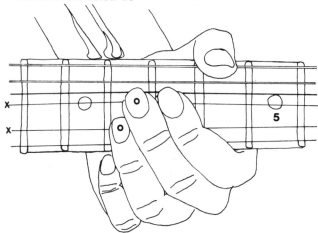

56

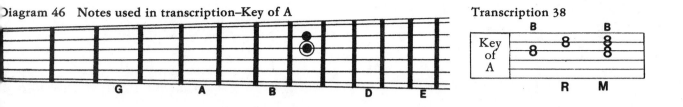

Diagram 46   Notes used in transcription–Key of A

Transcription 38

G   A   B   D   E

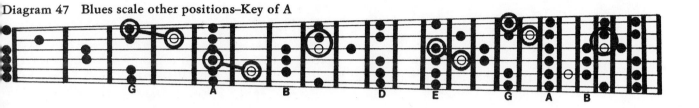

Diagram 47   Blues scale other positions–Key of A

G   A   B   D   E   G   A   B

Riff Five

With each riff there is a diagram labeled *other positions in the same key*. Riff five and six are the same riff explored in two different positions. For this reason both riffs will share the same *other positions* diagram.

Riff five uses the middle finger to bend the second string at the fourth fret to sound the note normally fretted on the fifth fret. The ring finger frets the first string at the fifth fret (root note fret).

Hand Illustration 11

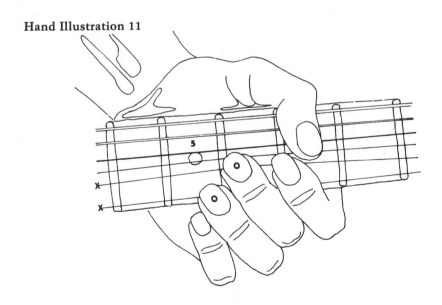

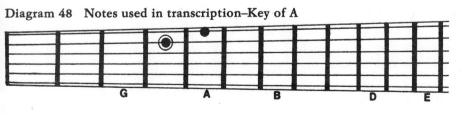

Diagram 48   Notes used in transcription–Key of A

G   A   B   D   E

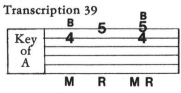

Transcription 39

57

Diagram 49 Blues scale other positions–Key of A

G   A   B   D   E   G   A   B

Riff Six

This riff is the same as riff five except it is positioned one octave lower along the root note fret pattern. The middle finger bends the fifth string at the sixth fret. The ring finger bends the fourth string at the seventh fret.

Hand Illustration 12

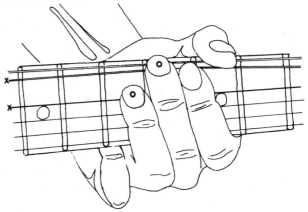

Diagram 50 Notes used in transcription–Key of A

G   A   B   D

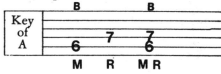

Transcription 40

Riff Seven

This is the sister riff to riff one. The ring finger bends the second string at the eigth fret to sound the note normally fretted two frets above on the tenth fret. This is the same note that is played by the index finger on the first string. You have to push this riff a bit harder than riff one in order to sound two identical notes because of the tuning difference between the strings. Concentrate on smoothly bending the note until it sounds precisely the note sounded by the index finger.

Hand Illustration 13

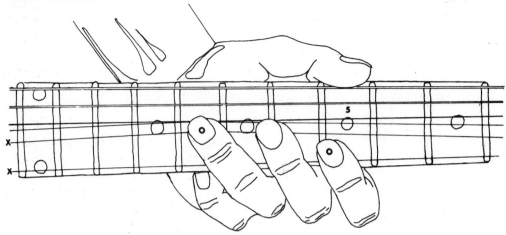

Diagram 51   Notes used in transcription–Key of A

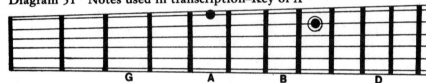

G   A   B   D

Transcription 41

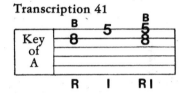

Diagram 52   Blues scale other positions–Key of A

G   A   B   D   E   G   A   B

Pulling

This section describes how the pulling technique is performed. With the index finger, fret the first two strings across the root note fret. The ring finger then frets the note three frets above the index on the first string and is plucked as usual. The ring finger then pulls or snaps off the string in such a way that the string is plucked by this action. This leaves the string ringing and the note held by the index finger is sounded *without being struck by the pick.*

Hand Illustration 14

This technique is widely used on many rock recordings. When you hear the guitarist *repeat* the same three, four or five note riff quickly and mechanically, he is most likely pulling notes. This technique is popular because it lets the amp do all the work and the guitarist can increase his speed of playing because he doesn't have to pick every note.

Riff Eight

This is a three note riff which pulls the first note. The index finger bars the first two strings at the root note fret. Pull the first note so the second note is sounded without the use of the pick.

Hand Illustration 15

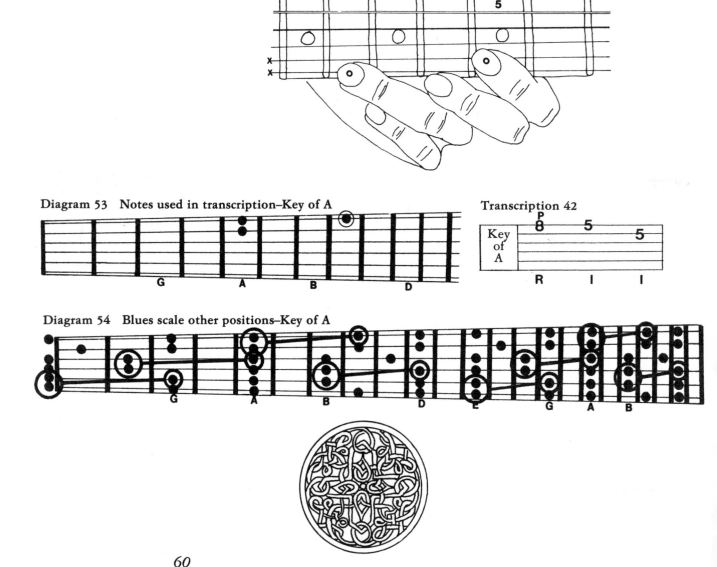

Diagram 53   Notes used in transcription–Key of A

Transcription 42

Diagram 54   Blues scale other positions–Key of A

Riff Nine

This three note riff also pulls the first note. The third note is a relative note held stationary by the middle finger. Remember, only the first and third notes are picked.

Hand Illustration 16

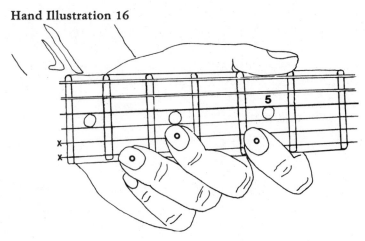

Diagram 55   Notes used in transcription–Key of A

Transcription 43

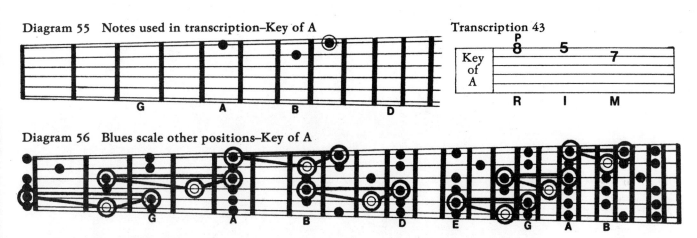

Diagram 56   Blues scale other positions–Key of A

These nine riffs are freely used to compose guitar leads of endless variation. They are to be mixed and matched and integrated into the various approaches from chapters 5 and 7. There is no standard way to play any of these. If you listen to a stack of records, you will hear them played over and over again as each artist lends his own special interpretation. This chapter is designed to open your eyes to the possibilities of the fretboard. It is now up to you to sit down with the scale patterns and explore.

Following are transcriptions which illustrate a few of the ways that the riffs can be used with other standard blues and relative notes along the root note fret.

Transcription 44

Chuck Berry was one of the first guitarists to use the bending of strings in a rock and roll style. Many of the bent note riffs shown above form the basics of his choppy, single note riff guitar style. The next example is an updated version of the riff which he invented and eventually became his trademark. This riff was used as an introduction to many of his twelve bar rock and roll songs and has been interpreted thousands of different ways by groups from the Rolling Stones to the Beatles.

The riff begins in the blues but after the second series of double notes, the riff goes into the relative scale. The index finger bars the first two strings at the fifth fret for the blues section but immediately after the second series of double notes, the index finger goes into position barring the first two strings at the second fret (the relative root note fret).

Joash lets fly the arrow of deliverance.

62

Transcription 45

Double Notes

Double note lead guitar riffs are commonly used in rock music. The outline of the blues pattern obviously lends itself to double note combinations. The example below is a study in the possibilities of double note combinations that occur at the same fret using notes from both basic scales.

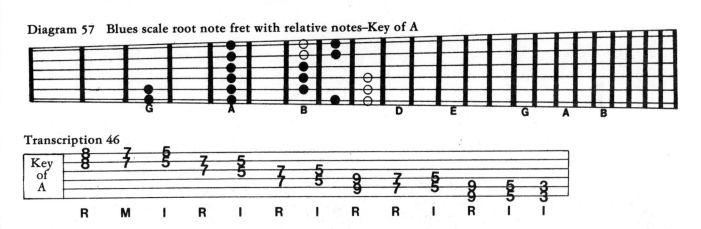

Diagram 57   Blues scale root note fret with relative notes—Key of A

Transcription 46

Riff Ten

Double note combinations can be substituted for a single note in the various *blues or mixed approaches*. Another effective technique is to bend a double note combination as if it were a single note. The following example bends a popular double note riff back and forth creating a vibrato effect.

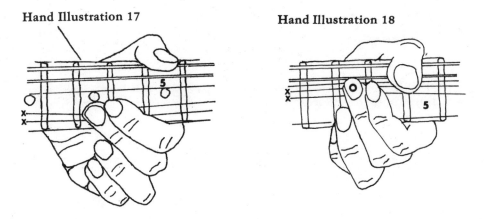

Hand Illustration 17   Hand Illustration 18

Diagram 58   Notes used in transcription–Key of A

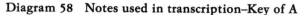

Transcription 47

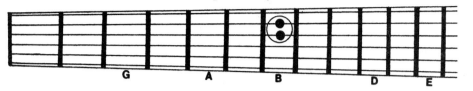

Riff Eleven

Double notes can also be played from two strings at different frets which fall into a chord or scale pattern. The possibilities for this type of combination are seemingly endless. The following example is a famous blues riff that can be used in any type of rock music. Try sliding both notes up to the position where they are illustrated.

Hand illustration 19

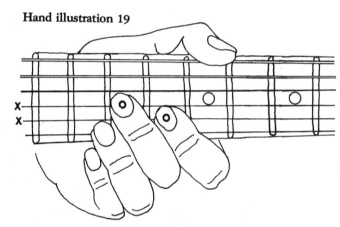

Diagram 59   Notes used in transcription–Key of A

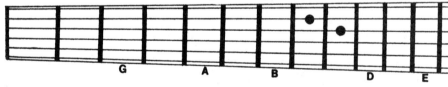

Transcription 48

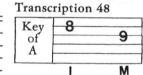

Diagram 60   Blues scale other positions–Key of A

The following example explores a combination of double notes taken from both the blues and the relative scale.

Transcription 49

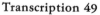

64

9
VERTICAL RIFFS

lthough most improvising is done along the root note fret or other linear patterns, there are also several possibilities for *movable* riffs that can be played vertically up or down the frets. You will become familiar with the unique sound of the vertical riffs the first time that you use them in practice. When movable riffs are used, varying string lengths create notes that change the character of the riff's sound as it progresses up or down. Working across the fret will give you approximately the same string length for a series of notes. Sliding techniques, such as moving a fretted, ringing note over another fret, are an integral part of using movables.

Transcription 50

Let's look at a preliminary single string study where a triplet moves down the high E string using the framework of the *blues in the Key of E* on the high E string. Fingering takes a priority in this example because of the long reach between frets as the scale moves down the fretboard. The transcription uses the index, middle and ring finger, however the pinky may be used if you find it more comfortable.

The movable chords diagrammed in the third chapter move up and down the fretboard with the root note of the chord corresponding to a chosen vertical pattern. The long narrow fretboard of the guitar lends itself to the movement of the left hand up or down the neck and the six strings allow the vertical movement of full chords, single notes, parts of chords or any movable note combination. This chapter explores the possibility of moving bent riffs and double note octave riffs vertically up and down the board.

The transcribed examples will demonstrate full fretboard use; however, when vertical riffs are employed in free improvising, they are often used only two or three at a time in conjunction with linear patterned scale riffs.

Octave Riffs

The following illustration visually demonstrates the possibilities for constructing pairs of notes which are one octave apart. *Octave riffs* are formed directly from standard major chord patterns, playing only the repeating octave notes while muting the other strings. Octave riffs have an interesting dual note sound that is often used by jazz guitarists for parts of the melody line.

The example below uses the *index finger on the sixth string at the root note fret* and the *ring finger two frets above the root fret on the fourth string.*

Hand Illustration 20

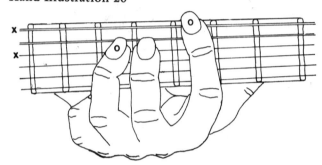

Diagram 61   Blues scale octave riff position–Key of A

Transcription 51

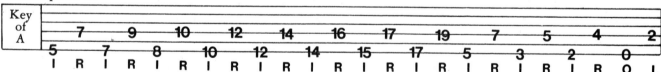

The second octave riff is derived from the G major chord. The *index finger* plays the *third string* on the *root note fret* while the *ring finger* plays the *first string three frets above the root note fret.* The three fret span above the root note fret in this example differs from the two note span in the previous example because of the tuning irregularity between the fourth and fifth string. Four half steps separate these strings while the rest are divided by five half steps.

66

Hand Illustration 21

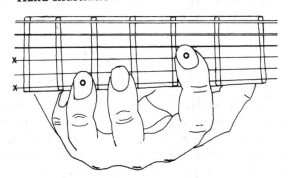

Diagram 62   Blues scale octave riff position–Key of A

Transcription 52

Movable Bent String Riffs

The bent string riffs that were explained in the previous chapter are also an excellent vehicle for moving up and down the board. These are double note riffs which use a bent note to sound two *identical* notes where the octave riffs use the same notes from different octaves.

The act of bending the string takes place at each different position where the riff is played. The first example uses the *ring finger* to bend *the third string three frets above the root note fret* until it sounds the note played by the *index finger on the second string on the root note fret.*

Hand Illustration 22

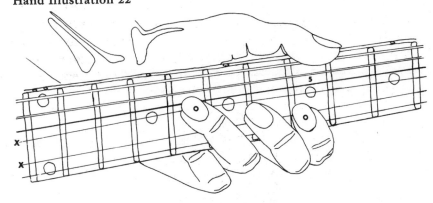

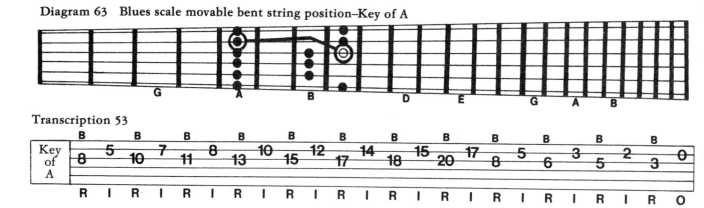

Diagram 63   Blues scale movable bent string position–Key of A

Transcription 53

The next example uses the *ring finger* to bend the *second string* on the *third fret above the root note fret* to sound the note played by the *index finger on the first string*.

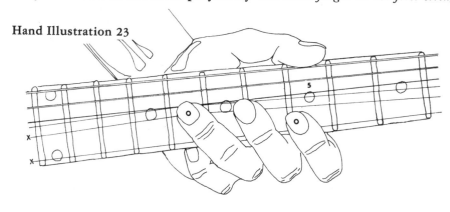

Hand Illustration 23

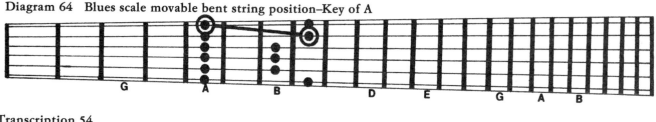

Diagram 64   Blues scale movable bent string position–Key of A

Transcription 54

The effectiveness of these riffs depends largely upon how the right hand is used to pluck the strings. Pick only the strings that are being fingered and experiment with different techniques. Certain recordings of Carlos Santana play the vertical bent string riffs by striking each position just once as if it were a single note. Moving the riff up or down the board, striking it once in each position, has a tremendous impact, a real power play.

Hendrix performed the same riff using the right hand to quickly repeat the notes of the riff, holding it for a set amount of time in each position. With sufficient help from the amp, this technique creates a constant, steady sound which is not found in the standard scale oriented riffs.

68

10
OFF
THE CHORD

elf taught artists are largely responsible for the various techniques of heavy guitar. Many styles evolved by simply letting the instrument lend itself to an idea, always yielding to an easier way to play a chord change or riff. Many lead guitar riffs result from playing the most accessible part of a scale pattern surrounding the chord pattern of a song. Songwriters get the chords down first, then work out the frills and hooks which distinguish the individual character of the song.

The complexity of the relationship between chords and scales can be approached by studying the major chords as they appear on and around the root note fret (Golden Rule). From there you can go on to explore the entire pattern. In order to get an idea of how many times any primary chord is repeated in the twelve note pattern, look to the final diagram in Chapter 12 which deals with chord inversion.

Rhythm Riff

One of the ways the notes around the chord are used directly with the chord is a rhythm guitar riff. This riff was made famous by Chuck Berry and represents the basic rock and roll idiom for the rhythm guitar. It is universally movable and can be recognized immediately in any of its many variations.

The basic riff is formed with the bottom two strings of an E chord with an additional relative note. The low E string is played open. The *index finger* is held stationary on the *fifth string, second fret* and the *ring finger* plays the *fifth string, fourth fret*. The rhythm alternates between the notes on the fifth string as shown in the following transcription.

This same riff can be played in the key of A by moving the entire process over to the fifth and fourth strings, being careful only to play those strings. The above riff is the most basic example of the rhythm riff. The method used by the right hand makes the difference in how the riff will sound. If each note is picked separately the resulting sound will be a slow blues rhythm. If both strings are played quickly with one movement of the pick, the riff can be a fast moving, solid background of sound. Here are two variations on the basic riff that uses notes on and around the root note fret.

Hand Illustration 24

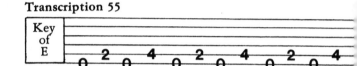

Diagram 65   E major chord with relative note

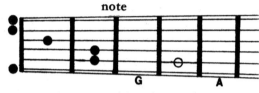

Transcription 55

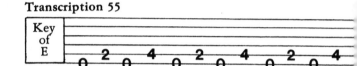

Transcription 56

Movable Rhythm Riff

The rhythm riff is a *movable*, versatile riff when it is applied to bar chords using both the E and A major. In order to form the movable riff, place the index finger at the desired root note fret on the low E string. The root note will determine the chord you are using as a base. The middle finger is held stationary on the fifth string on the second fret above the root note fret and the ring finger is used to alternately tap the fifth string at the fourth fret above the root note fret.

Hand Illustration 25

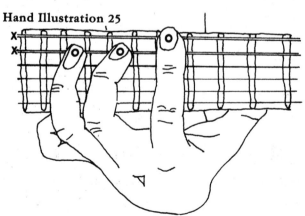

Once you understand and play this movable riff, reread the section on understanding the structure of rock songs and play the twelve bar blues using the movable rhythm riff. Here is an example to give insight into how this riff moves. The major chord sequence is C, G, D and A and was used by Keith Richard for the chorus of *Jumping Jack Flash* (it's aaaaaaalll riiiiiight now).

Transcription 57

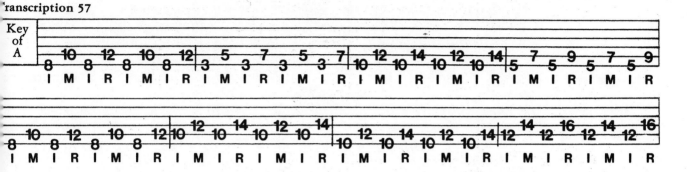

Repeating Riffs

Many rock and blues songs are based around a single riff that repeats itself throughout the changes of the chords through the song. These riffs invariably use part of the root chord in their structure. Here is an example of a *repeating blues riff* taken off the chord. Each riff is played in the three positions of the twelve bar blues.

Transcription 58

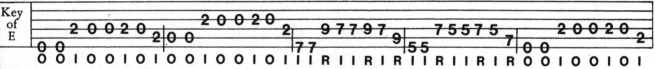

The previous example may have reminded you of bass guitar lines which could be used for any blues based song. Of course the bass guitar, having the same notes as the four bottom strings of a six string an octave lower, is integrated with lead guitar. The next twelve bar example could be considered a *line* which uses the notes of the major chord. The major chord from which the borrowed notes are taken is noted in the transcription.

Transcription 59

71

Parts of Chords

The real potential of using parts of a chord as a riff is often overlooked because of the simplicity of the idea. One, two or three notes of any chord can be played in any number of combinations. When the music of the great blues guitarists is analysed note for note, it is found to be a combination of the two basic five note scales and parts of chord configurations known as inversions.

The bent note riff that was explored in *Heavy Riffs* (chapter 8), is composed of notes in the root chord. The movable double octave riffs from the previous chapter are composed of the root note of the major chord.

Any chord can be used to construct ideas for the lead guitar. The following example shows how *two notes* can be picked out of a full chord to create a lead pattern. The transcription follows the E7th chord barred at the seventh fret, fifth fret, and the open position. The final two notes are taken from a B7th chord in the open position at the bottom of the board. The chord sequence is B, A, E and B. Circled notes are used in the transcription as movable units.

Diagram 66   E seventh chord   Diagram 67   B seventh chord

Transcription 60

Key of E																					

72

The next two examples illustrate how the notes of the chord itself can be used in the fabric of lead work.

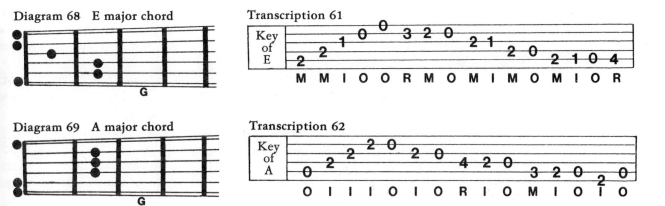

Diagram 68   E major chord

Transcription 61

Diagram 69   A major chord

Transcription 62

Please explore. Listen very closely to the lead guitar work on recordings and you will soon be able to identify practically any technique. You can pick the individual notes of a chord to form part of the linear series of notes (known as broken chords) or you can strum several strings and leave them ringing while you move into single notes.

The first three notes of the next example are the top three strings of an E bar chord at the fifth fret (A Chord). The fourth note is the same as the third but is a lead note to be played hard with lots of vibrato. Then we change to the movable 9th chord (root note fifth string) which is to be strummed once followed quickly by lead work from below the root note fret.

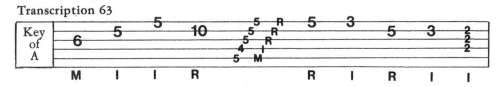

Transcription 63

Now aren't you glad that you have practiced all of the blues and relative approaches until you can visualize them in any position? Now the trick is to find the most convenient positions to execute smooth licks. Note how nicely the three fretted notes of the A major chord, and the notes of the D chord, match up with the root fret of the A relative scale.

Diagram 70   Relative scale–Key of A   Diagram 71   D major chord   Diagram 72   A major chord

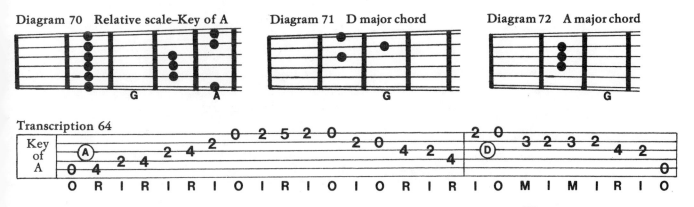

Transcription 64

73

The purpose of the Heavy Guitar Bible is to present all of the information you will need for further study of the fretboard. The twelve chapters and appendix give a high impact presentation which covers a lot of ground. Examples of guitar work are very carefully chosen to shed light on the text, but are only intended to be model exercises. The book moves directly to the next subject leaving you with the responsibility of providing your own explorations. The Bible just knocks over the first domino.

Let's quickly review the possibilities for chord/scale combination. This book presents the blues scale in a twelve note repeating pattern along with the relative, major, composite and other scales. Also included are the major chords with their minors, sevenths, sixths and ninths which can be played in several positions. What this means, if you are really going to play off the chord, is a hell of a lot of homework for you. The most important thing to keep in mind is that all of these relationships occur simultaneously and constantly and that it is the human mind that picks out singular channels for use.

Chords and scales blend together when we listen to a few hours of rock music. Incredible scale application: listen to Jeff Beck's *Blow by Blow.* Beautiful leadwork: try *The Wind Cries Mary* on Hendrix's first album. Disciplined blues lead: Mick Taylor with the Stones on *Get Your Ya Ya's Out* or Johnny Winter's *Nothing But the Blues.* Chords? Pete Townshend's *Tommy.* It goes on and on.

Don't be overcome by the possibilities. Although technical knowledge is necessary, never let it get in the way of expression. Don't struggle with the instrument, just ponder all of the dimensions and rest assured that if you keep exploring, all of the facts will fit into one total pattern.

11
SCALE EXPO

he blues and the relative are the two fundamental scales used by rock guitarists. There are, however, several other scales that have come into common use as the electric guitar expands into different types of music. The fifties introduced the basics and the late sixties pushed the basics to their limits, but the seventies have seen the electric guitar applied to an entire spectrum of new possibilities, which could only have evolved after decades of intense development. Jazz rock or Fusion music uses the guitar's fretboard in the same light as a saxophone or lead piano, which means adapting all of the scales used by jazz artists for use with the contemporary electric guitar.

Chapters 11 and 12 have a different direction than the other chapters in the book. They are designed to offer you a broad base of knowledge so you can apply yourself to the musical direction which you choose. This chapter introduces the major scale and explores several of the combinations in which it can be used, while introducing the reader to the huge number of scale combinations and derivatives made possible by the major scale. For a reference point, let's review the blues and relative scale in the key of A.

Diagram 73   Blues scale–Key of A

Diagram 74   Relative scale–Key of A

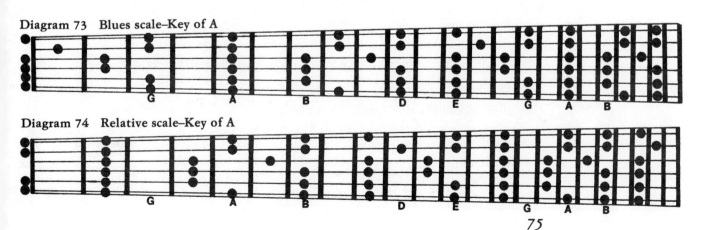

The Major Scale

The major scale is the seven note doe, ray, me scale that is familiar to everybody. The seven notes, which are chosen from the twelve notes of the octave, form a unique pattern as they climb up the scale. The major scale can be approached for study in the same way as the blues and the relative. Just as any scale, the major scale has a specific twelve fret repeating pattern which can be broken down into convenient boxes which are the easiest to finger. Below is an example of the major scale in the key of A diagrammed only on the A string. The A string plucked open will sound the primary key or tonic note.

Diagram 75   Notes of major scale on A string–Key of A

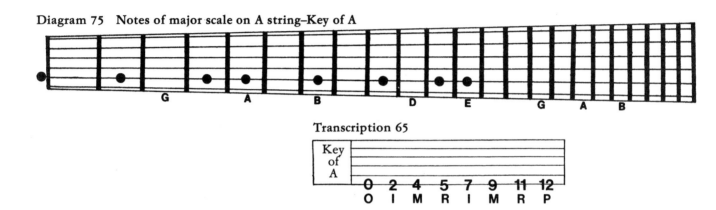

Transcription 65

The distance between any two notes is called an interval. This distance can be counted by using half steps (one fret), whole steps (two frets) or by simply stating the number of frets. Any scale can be defined by stating the intervals between the notes of the scale (scale degrees). For instance, the seven note major scale has an interval sequence of whole step, whole step, half step, whole step, whole step, whole step, half step (see diagram below).

The keyboard of the piano is modeled after the major scale in the key of C. The white notes represent the seven notes of the major scale (the seven notes between A and G) and the black notes are the five flats or sharps grouped in sets of two and three (see diagram 1).

Each of the notes of the major scale has its own particular tonal characteristics. After conscientious practice, the special traits of each note can be recognized and you can go on to study the finer points of their interrelationship. Each of the seven notes has its own formal name which is demonstrated in the chart below. The most popular method for identification of the major scale degree is the simple number system which assigns the number 1 to the first key note of the scale, and progresses evenly from that point. The numbers 8 and 9 are often used to designate the first and second notes from the next higher octave. The number system is the easiest most universal way to go and is used in the designation of complex chords (sixth, seventh, ninth etc.) which is explained in the next chapter.

The *fourth* and the *fifth* notes of the major scale directly correspond with the *second*, and the *third* basic chords used for the twelve bar blues progression, five and seven frets above the root note fret. The phrase *going to the fifth* means playing the third change in the twelve bar blues. In the key of E, the fifth would be a B note or chord.

76

Diagram 76 Major scale chart

Number	1	2	3	4	5	6	7	8
Common Name	Doe	Ray	Me	Fa	So	La	Te	Doe
Formal Name	Tonic	Supertonic	Mediant	Subdominant	Dominant	Submediant or Superdominant	Leading Tone or Subtonic	Tonic
Interval	●	●	●	●	●	●	●	●
Whole (W) Half (H)		W	W	H	W	W	W	H

There are many interesting facts concerning the individual notes of the major scale. The third and the seventh, the two notes which take their place a half step below the following note, are often called leading tones because they conveniently move toward the next degree. The most important tones are the tonic, dominant and subdominant. There is a strong relationship between the tonic and the dominant (the first and fifth) and the major chord is composed of the first, the third and the fifth. The next chapter, *Building,* will explain chord construction.

Now let's look at the complete pattern created by the major scale in the key of A as it appears on the entire fretboard on all six strings.

Diagram 77   Major scale boxes–Key of A

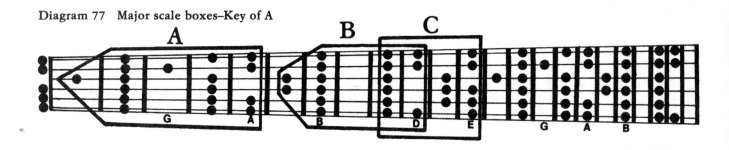

This pattern is far more complex than the five note pattern of the blues or the relative. The basic five note pattern has only one *root note fret* where notes from the scale appear on all six strings simultaneously across one fret. When using the blues scale, the root note fret helps to visually orient the guitarist because it is determined by the position of the key root note on the low E string.

The major scale pattern has *three* frets where the notes of the scale appear on each string across a given fret, *none of which* take place on the fret where the key note appears on the low E string. These three positions are the most common places to approach playing the major scale. Let's go through each one.

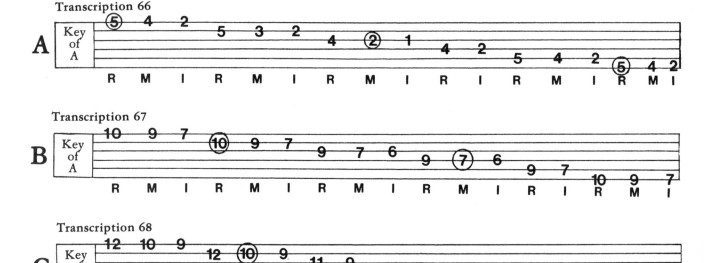

The major scale naturally lends itself to a melodic flow of notes. It can be studied in the same way as the blues scale was in the *Blues Approaches*. The scale can be practiced with the use of a vehicle unit which contains a certain number of notes, which works its way up through the octave.

The next example shows position C in the key of C. This example conveniently uses the open strings with notes from the first three frets. The first part of the transcription simply moves through the scale. The second part breaks the scale down into four note units.

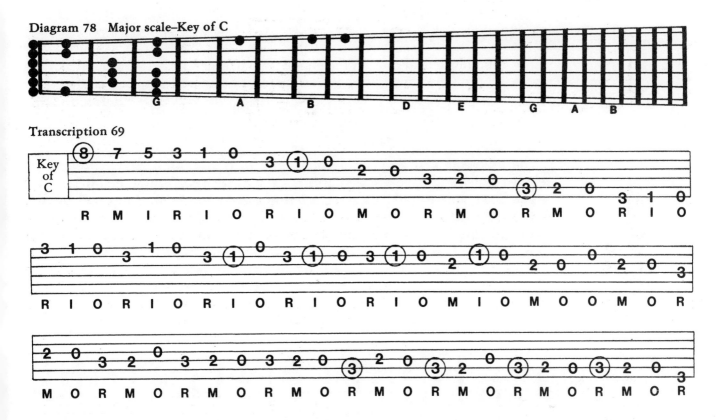

Diagram 78   Major scale–Key of C

Transcription 69

Minor Scales

Next we will look at the minor scale series. Minor scales are built from the major scale by lowering selected notes by one half step. There are several different modes of the minor, each of which contain a different selection of diminished notes. The diagram below shows the *natural mode*, which diminishes the third, the sixth and the seventh of the major scale resulting in an interval pattern of W, H, W, W, H, W, W (W = whole step, H = half step).

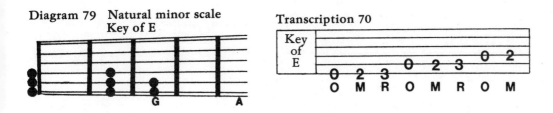

Diagram 79   Natural minor scale
Key of E

Transcription 70

The next example diagrams the *harmonic mode* of the minor scale which is identical to the natural mode except that it does not diminish the seventh of the major scale.

79

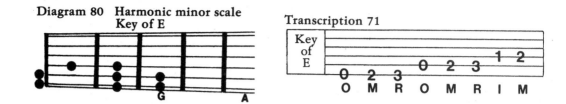

Diagram 80 Harmonic minor scale
Key of E

Transcription 71

The complete chord chart at the end of this chapter contains an example of the *melodic* minor scale which has both an ascending and a descending mode.

Composite Scales

The following scales are composed of notes taken from both the blues and relative scales and have a scale pattern which is identical to the major scale.

The first scale we shall look at has a definite place in both rock music and jazz. It is the major scale for G when the music is in the key of A. This seven note scale will fit directly into place along the root note fret in the key of A. Does the pattern look familiar? It is the blues scale pattern with two relative notes or the golden rule with the omission of one note. This major scale is diagrammed only along the root note fret for playing in the key of A (fifth fret). This position corresponds with position B of the major scale breakdown from diagram 77.

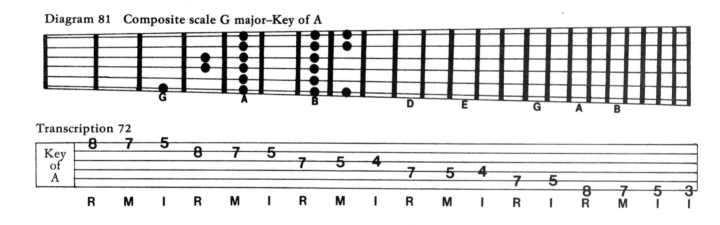

Diagram 81 Composite scale G major–Key of A

Transcription 72

Just as the above scale was formed by adding two relative notes to the blues scale, the next example is made by adding two blues notes to the complete relative scale. This is the major scale in the key of D for music played in the key of A. This position corresponds with position C of the major chord study from diagram 77.

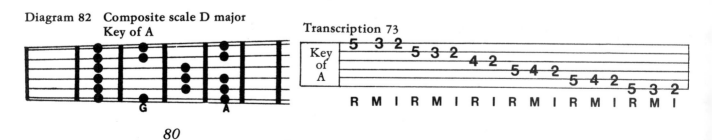

Diagram 82 Composite scale D major
Key of A

Transcription 73

We are moving very fast through some very important material. Let's take a short verbal review. First of all we have the eight notes from the combination of the blues and relative scale which form the outline of the *Golden Rule* . The seven note major scale has been found to fit into three positions for use in any key. For use in the key of A, the major scale pattern can be centered in the key of D, G and of course, the key of A. These positions offer you more than a new technique within the usual patterns. They propose a new framework. The first time I tried out the various major scale positions when I was jamming, the other guitarist immediately looked over and said, "What in the world was that, I never heard you do that before." I said, "It's the major in some removed key, can you *believe it!*"

The final composite scale presented below is the relative scale with the addition of a single melodic note from the major scale. The addition of this unique note, which is the fourth of the major scale and is circled in the diagram, adds a smooth touch to leads using the straight relative scale. This special six note scale could also be considered the major scale with the omission of the seventh scale degree.

Diagram 83   Composite relative scale
              Key of A

Transcription 74

SCALE CHART

The thirteen numbers across the top of the chart represent the twelve notes of the octave plus an added first above the twelfth. The use of numbers to represent the twelve units of the octave at one half step intervals is the most basic way in which they can be presented. The chart is set up to show all scales in the key of C because the letters (A through G) were traditionally layed out to fit the Key of C. The most important concept behind scale construction is the interval pattern, and if you keep this in mind it is easy to transpose any scale to any key by putting the tonic note relative to number one. For instance, the|major scale could be represented by this series of numbers for use as an interval pattern for any key: 1, 3, 5, 6, 8, 10, 12, 13. The octave of the first is indicated by a prime notation (').

The *chromatic scale* is every note in the octave and chromatic scale runs are characterized by a series of notes which are only one half step apart from each other. The *whole note scale* is a climb up the ladder of the octave, starting on the number one or tonic, using a whole step (two fret) interval.

Diagram 84   Scale chart

Numbers	1	2	3	4	5	6	7	8	9	10	11	12	1
Chromatic	C	C#	D	D#	E	F	F#	G	G#	A	A#	B	C'
Whole Note	C		D		E		F#		G#		A#		C'
Blues	C			D#		F		G			A#		C'
Relative	C		D		E			G		A			C'
Major	C		D		E	F		G		A		B	C'
Minor Modes													
Natural	C		D	D#		F		G	G#		A#	B	C'
Melodic Ascending	C		D	D#		F		G		A		B	C'
Melodic Descending	C		D	D#		F		G	G#		A#		C'
Harmonic	C		D	D#		F		G	G#			B	C'

82

12
BUILDING

Alright, now we are going to tie this whole thing together. Music is an art and a science. It does not matter if you are a full tilt heavy metal axe wielder or a classical violinist, you are basically dealing with the same elements. The nature of this chapter is a bit different than the others because it aims to paint a structural picture rather than give technique examples.

There really is a total picture to the fabric of music which is similar to the guidelines of any practical science. Humans found the patterns to exist but did not actually design them. Music was waiting.

Many different kinds of musicians will read this book and some may feel that they don't need to know anything more formal about music than they now know. For certain types of blues and rock it may not be necessary to fully understand the instrument. Even if you don't think you will apply any more theory, you are invited along for an interesting ride. You may be very surprised at exactly what you have been doing all along.

The seventies has opened up the electric guitar to a vast spectrum of adaptation. In order to understand its true versatility, it is necessary to realize the full potential of the instrument. Take your time and read things twice and three times if you don't understand immediately and refer the ideas of the text to the charts provided. You will find that the fretboard is ready when you are.

Intervals

The difference in pitch between two notes is known as an *interval*. On the guitar, an interval of one fret represents a *half step* which is the smallest interval common to our musical system. The *whole step* is an interval of two frets and there are twelve half steps or six whole steps to an octave. If two notes are sounded successively, the interval is known as *melodic*, but if both notes are sounded at the same time, the result is a *harmonic* interval.

The major scale is derived from the twelve notes of the octave and has an interval pattern as diagrammed below. The key of C is used for all examples unless otherwise noted. Whole Step = W, Half Step = H.

Diagram 85 Major scale intervals

Interval		W	W	H	W	W	W	H
Major Scale Letter Name		C	D	E	F	G	A	B
Major Scale Number Name		1	2	3	4	5	6	7

The name given to an interval is taken from the number of scale degrees (the notes in the scale) involved from the lower note to the higher. Using the tonic or first scale degree as the first note (in this case a C note), resulting intervals will take the same name as the scale degree number of the second note. For instance, the interval between a C note and a D note (the second note of the scale) is a second. The interval between a C note and an E note (third note of the scale) is a third and so on up to the B note which is a seventh. *Simple* intervals are less than an octave while *compound* intervals span more than an octave. Numbers greater than seven present compound intervals. An interval *complements* another if the sum of their scale degree numbers adds up to eight (one octave). The word *lower* is used to describe the downward movement of an interval. For instance, the lower second of C is a B note.

The numerical references, second, third, etc., are used to describe intervals even if they do not originate on the first of the scale. Let's look at the interval between the third and the sixth notes of the C major scale.

$$\text{C D } \overset{3}{\text{E}} \text{ F G } \overset{6}{\text{A}} \text{ B C'}$$

Because this interval includes four scale degrees, it is a fourth. This leaves us with a rather complex situation. Because of the way the major scale was selected from the octave using both whole and half steps, two different intervals may include the same number of scale degrees but actually span a different number of frets. For instance, the intervals C to E and D to F are both thirds but the former is four half steps and the latter is three half steps. In order to accommodate all of these variables, a system exists which categorizes all possible intervals. Although all of that information is not presented here, the common name for intervals between one and twelve half steps is provided by the chart below.

The information in the first two columns is universal and pertains to intervals starting on any given note. For instance, an A note is five frets (five half steps) above an E note, so A is a perfect fifth above E.

Please note this distinguishing point: if an interval is described in one word (a second, a fifth, or a seventh), the interval spans a specific number of *major scale degrees* above an indicated note. However, if the interval is described in two words (a major second, a perfect fifth, or a minor seventh), the interval specifies a certain number of *half steps* between two indicated notes.

Triads

A *triad* is a chord which consists of three tones or notes. The three notes which make a triad are the fundamental note from which the chord takes its letter name and two other notes which are separated from the fundamental by a third and a

Diagram 86   Common intervals

Number of Half Steps in Interval	Formal Name of Interval	Abbreviated Name or Symbol	Chromatic Scale Key of C	Major Scale Degree in Key of C
0	Unison or Prime	Octave	C	1
1	Minor Second	m2	C#	
2	Major Second	M2	D	2
3	Minor Third	m3	D#	
4	Major Third	M3	E	3
5	Perfect Fourth	P4	F	4
6	Diminished Fifth	Dim 5	F#	
7	Perfect Fifth	P5	G	5
8	Minor Sixth	m6	G#	
9	Major Sixth	M6	A	6
10	Minor Seventh	m7	A#	
11	Major Seventh	M7	B	7
12	Octave	0'	C'	8

fifth respectively. In other words, a triad is a series of three notes with an interval of a third between the first note and the second and also between the second and third.

There are four different types of triads, *major, minor, diminished* and *augmented*. The type of triad is determined by two factors: whether the thirds used are major thirds or minor thirds, and the sequence in which these thirds are used. Below is a chart containing details about the four basic triads and how they are constructed.

Diagram 87   Triad chart

Type of Triad	First Note	First Interval	Second Interval	Example in C
Major Triad	Fundamental Note	Major Third	Minor Third	C-E-G
Minor Triad	Fundamental Note	Minor Third	Major Third	C-D#-G
Diminished Triad	Fundamental Note	Minor Third	Minor Third	C-D#-F#
Augmented Triad	Fundamental Note	Major Third	Major Third	C-E-G#

Common Chords

The third chapter of this book, *Chords and Structure,* introduced the fact that for any given key there are *three basic chords* used in blues structure and further explained that *each of the three basic chords has a relative minor chord.* These six common chords can be *built* directly from the components of the major scale. The Major scale in the key of C uses the notes C D E F G A B C: If triads are built using each of the seven notes of the scale as the fundamental note of a triad, using thirds as

intervals, there is an interesting result. Rather than seven letter name notes, w[e]
now have seven different chords. In the key of C, the resulting chords would b[e]

Diagram 88   Common chords–Key of C

C major, D minor, E minor, F major, G major, A minor, and B diminished.

The three basic blues chords in the key of C are *C, F and G major* and their relativ[e]
minors are *A, D and E minor.* The diminished chord is derived from the seventh [of]
the scale is another related chord. It is in this way that the basic chord system [is]
derived from the major scale for use in any key.

Building Chords

From the section on triads, we have already seen how major, minor, augmente[d]
and diminished chords are constructed. All of the other universally used chord[s]
are constructed using one of these four triads and additional notes in relation t[o]
the major scale.

The following chord chart gives the formula that is used to derive the common[ly]
used chords from the major scale. The common triads are determined by interv[al]
formulas. For example, the major chord is the first, the third and the fifth of th[e]
major scale. In order to form a minor chord, the third is diminished by one ha[lf]
step.

Scale degree numbers are often used to name common triads with the additio[n]
of one extra major scale note. The major sixth chord is the three notes of th[e]
major triad with the addition of the sixth from the scale. The minor sixth chord [is]
the same as the major sixth chord with a flatted third. When a number great[er]

an 7 is used in a chord name it means that a scale degree is being used from the next octave above the fundamental note. For instance, a ninth chord uses the second from the next octave above the primary octave. Also note that any chord named with a number above 7 also includes the flatted seventh which is placed between the fifth of the scale and the named note. The chords with a plus number (+) simply add that scale degree to the named chord.

Diagram 89   Chord building

Chord Name	Scale degrees of successive notes					
Major	1	3	5			
Minor	1	b3	5			
Dominant 7th or 7th	1	3	5	b7		
Major 7th (ma7)	1	3	5	7		
Minor 7th (m7)	1	b3	5	b7		
Augmented (+)	1	3	#5			
Diminished	1	b3	b5			
Major 6th	1	3	5	6		
Major 6th	1	3	5	6		
9th	1	3	5	b7	9	
11th	1	3	5	b7	9	11
Major add 9 (+ 9)	1	3	5	9		
Minor 9th (m9)	1	b3	5	b7	9	
Major 6/9th	1	3	5	6	9	

The augmented and diminished chords are called "altered" because they have chromatically altered notes in their construction. The major chord or triad is considered to be "consonant", which means it creates a pleasant or stable sound effect. All other chords are called dissonant which produces tension and calls to be resolved by movement towards the major chord. Series of notes which have seconds for intervals are also used in certain types of music and are referred to as tone clusters."

Inversion

Inversion is a procedure in which an existing note is replaced by the same note taking its place in a higher or lower octave. A simple interval is inverted by substituting the lower tone into the next higher octave. For example, the inversion of the interval E-G would be G-E'.

The major triad has two forms of inversion. The *first inversion* places the fundamental note into the next higher octave and positions it after the fifth scale degree. The *second inversion* places both the fundamental and the third into the next octave and plays the fifth of the major scale first. For example, in the key of C the major triad is C-E-G. The first inversion would be E-G-C' while the second inversion would be G-C'-E'.

By this time you may well be saying, "What the hell does this have to do with me and my guitar?" Well, we are getting to that. An inversion could loosely be defined as another place to play the same chord. In order to take command of the fretboard, it is best to know all of the chords in all of their positions. The diagram below will give you a good foothold for understanding just how the same major chord appears in different inversions all over the fretboard. The interesting thing about the diagram is that all of the standard major chord configurations are shown to appear up and down the board as inversions for a single major chord.

That's right, all of the chords that you first learned at the top of the board using open strings (e.g. C major, A major, D major) only represent the most convenient selection from a twelve note pattern which contains all major chord patterns. This pattern is adjusted to the key of the major scale from which the major chord is derived.

Diagram 90 Common chord inversion

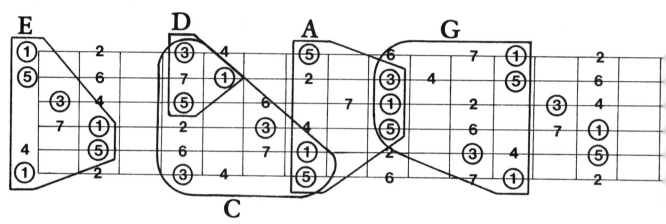

Here is how the diagram was made. The seven notes of the major scale in the key of E were placed on all six strings and numbered by scale degree. In order to highlight the components of the major scale, the first, third and fifth scale degree were circled. The most identifiable major chord configurations were then outlined with a line border and identified by letter. This pattern can be transposed by placing the tonic note of the scale (the circled number one) on the chosen note on the low E string. Please note that all chords in the diagram are E major chords and the designation of the other name chords are only for identifying their most familiar configuration.

APPENDIX

Richard

1 ✽ FINGERING

The most fundamental fingering exercise is the *one fret per finger* climb starting on the low E string and playing the notes on the first four frets, consecutively using the index, middle, ring and pinky. Counting the open string there will be five notes played on each string. These exercises are for limbering up all of your fingers and if done regularly they will lend speed to your playing and increase your dexterity.

Hand illustration 26

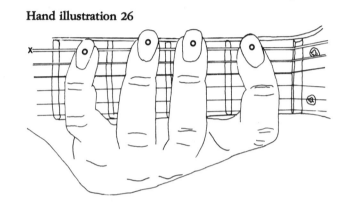

Transcription 75

Two additional finger exercises.

Transcription 76

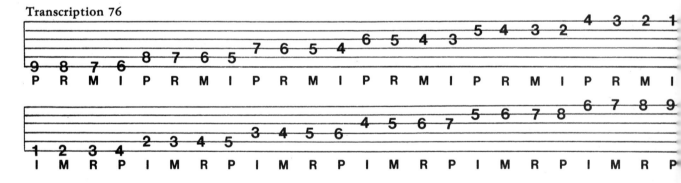

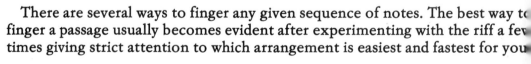

There are several ways to finger any given sequence of notes. The best way to finger a passage usually becomes evident after experimenting with the riff a few times giving strict attention to which arrangement is easiest and fastest for you.

The Pinky

The great majority of riffs that result from using the basic five note scales can be easily executed using just the ring and index finger and this is a great way to become familiar with the scales and basic rock guitar fingering technique. The us

90

of the little finger, however, can open up a new world of possibilities. If we look closely at the left hand of the great guitarists we will see that they use their little finger with the same dexterity as the other fingers. This can seem incredible to the beginner or to those who never developed the use of their pinkies. It is best to develop use of the pinky early. Here is an easy example. It uses the pinky instead of the standard ring finger arrangement. The index finger moves across the root note fret.

Transcription 77

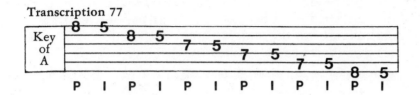

This substitution example may wake you up to how much pinky control you possess. Progress comes fast for those that are enthusiastic. The pinky can be a tremendous asset when it comes to those fine touches and little gimmicks that make the difference between average and true class. The pinky is widely used in chording, but the secret is to develop its use for fretting or hammering strings one or two frets above notes fretted by the other fingers.

Passages which involve the seven note major scale or a combination of the five note scales are more likely to require complex fingering and greater dexterity.

2 ◦ PICKING THE NOTE

Initially, there are three possibilities for picking a single note: the down stroke, the up stroke and alternate up and down strokes. Sure, this seems simple, but give picking some consideration. The role of the right hand in developing a versatile style has often been overlooked. To get an idea of how versatile you are with your right hand, try picking the blues scale along the root note fret using each of the three above methods.

The up stroke of the pick creates a distinctly different sound than the down stroke. The up stroke has a piercing, sharp sound. A four or five note riff that is played with just up strokes has a unique treble sound. Plucking the string very close to the bridge will also result in a sharper, higher pitched sound.

If it is speed that you want, you should be able to use the alternate picking style integrally with the other styles. For practice, go through the blues scale picking each note 4, 6 or 8 times alternately up and down before moving on to the next note in the sequence.

An interesting trick that has come into practice is plucking and immediately muting the string with the tip of the thumb. This is done by holding the pick tight and picking down on the string so that the thumb touches the string immediately after the pick. This technique works best at higher volume levels and leaves a singing harmonic sound ringing from the muted string similar to those produced by an out of phase switch wired into quality guitars.

3 ❀ SLIDING

Sliding is a simple technique where the note is played in one of the following ways:
- The string is plucked while it is fretted one or two frets below the desired note. The finger then slides the ringing note up to the proper fret.
- The string is plucked while it is fretted above the desired fret. The finger then slides down the string and holds the note at the desired fret.
- A combination of both the slide up and the slide down. This combination of techniques usually takes place over the distance of only one fret.

The sliding technique can also be used on entire chords or any parts of chords.

4 ❀ THE HAMMER

The hammer is used frequently in all forms of rock and blues. Here are three ways in which the hammer is commonly used.
- To hammer on, a note is fretted, usually with the index finger, and is plucked as usual. Another finger is then sharply brought down on the string at a higher fret.
- To hammer off, the second note from the above example is plucked and the finger is quickly removed to sound the note held by the index finger below.
- To repeat hammer, the two techniques above are repeated on two notes to produce a continuous sound without plucking.

5 ❀ VIBRATO

Any movement on a string after it has been sounded will change the character of the note. Vibrato is the rocking of the finger on the string to create a variating tone. This oscillation of the note is subtle, especially when compared to the bending technique where the string is moved across the fret.

There are two popular types of vibrato. One results from movement of the finger itself and is often known as the trill. The other comes from the rocking movement of the wrist back and forth in the direction of the neck. A guitarist's personal style is expressed in his vibrato.

Hand Illustration 27

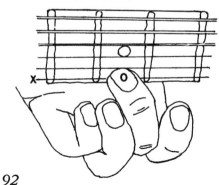

Hand Illustration 28

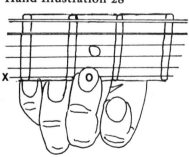

92

B.B. King said it took a good part of his life to perfect his vibrato to the point where it became his personal signature. Vibrato is usually developed when the musican becomes familiar with the other techniques and can concentrate on the finer details of guitar style. Johnny Winter said, "I can tell if I like a person's style after listening to his vibrato for ten seconds."

6 ✤ FILLER NOTES

Sometimes you will hear a guitarist play notes that don't fit exactly into any scale pattern, but sound in place with the scale framework being used. Most likely you are hearing notes that are located immediately between notes of the scale proper and are being used as chromatic steps for movement between scale degrees. These notes are not prominently sounded but used only as fillers to create a smooth transition between notes. Let's look at an example of where these notes are located relative to the blues scale in the key of E.

Tim

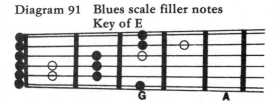

Diagram 91   Blues scale filler notes
Key of E

Transcription 78

The A ♯ note from the above example is the most commonly used filler note and is located on the first fret, second string and the third fret, third string. This note is often considered by blues piano players to be an integral part of the blues scale.

7 ✤ DIFFERENT PLACES

Unlike the instruments that play only one note at a time, the six strings of a guitar lend themselves to repeating scale and chord patterns which present lots of position possibilities. Each different area of the fretboard has its own characteristic sound qualities, and by forcing yourself to explore new positions you will become familiar with the sound particular to each region.

The same riff can be played in different octaves producing two riffs of distinctively varied pitch and fingering sequence.

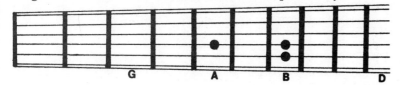

Diagram 92   Blues scale notes used in transcription–Key of A

Transcription 79

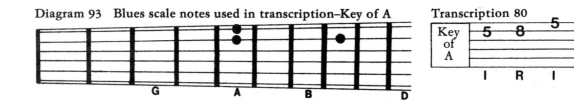

Diagram 93   Blues scale notes used in transcription–Key of A

Transcription 80

It is also possible to play the same riff in different positions in the same octave. Note the variance in tone quality between the two positions in the example below.

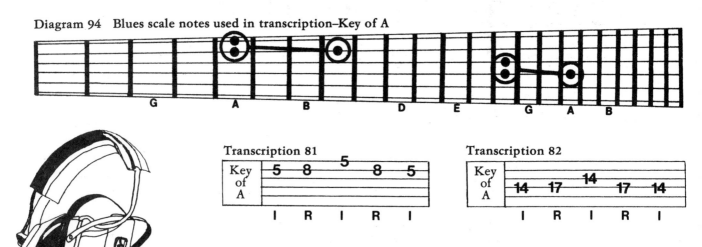

Diagram 94   Blues scale notes used in transcription–Key of A

Transcription 81

Transcription 82

It is always important to consider the possibilties of fingering a single riff in a variety of ways, particularly if you are copying a record or tape. The next example transcribes the same riff, a double triplet , using two different arrangements.

The first arrangement takes its place *above* the root note fret within the pattern of the *Golden Rule*.

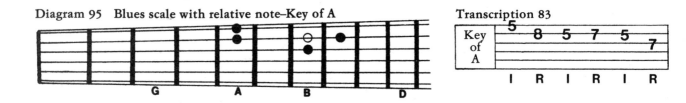

Diagram 95   Blues scale with relative note–Key of A

Transcription 83

A second arrangement takes its position *below* the root note fret. The advantage of this position is that the first note of the riff can be pulled, sounding the note held by the index finger without it actually being plucked.

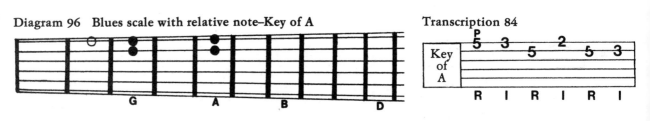

Diagram 96   Blues scale with relative note–Key of A

Transcription 84

94

The following double note vertical riff is transcribed in two different positions in the key of E.

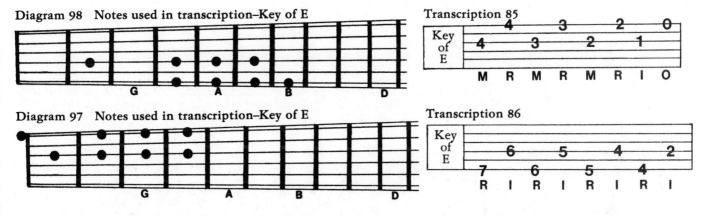

Diagram 98   Notes used in transcription–Key of E

Transcription 85

Diagram 97   Notes used in transcription–Key of E

Transcription 86

Remember that any riff or chord change can be fingered in a variety of positions to create different musical effects.

8 ❀ BLUES REVIEW

This section of the appendix reviews the blues scale in the key of E and A. Practicing the scale using the transcriptions below will help you to envision the entire pattern. It will also turn you on to a few new approaches that are not shown elsewhere in the book.

Transcription 87

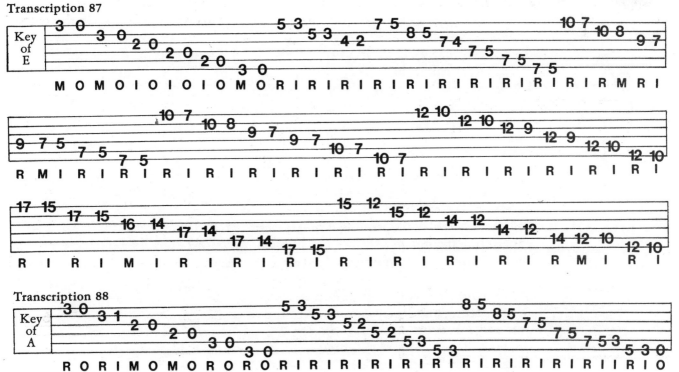

Transcription 88

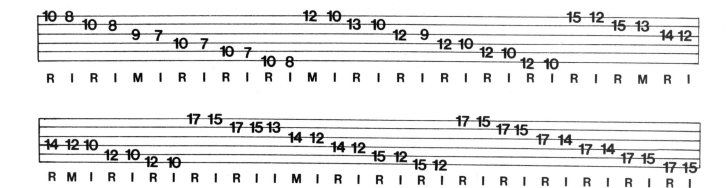

9 ❀ THE POWER PLAY

During the early development of the modern electric guitar, the guitar played a minor role in the music produced by the musicians on the bandstand. When the electric guitar came into its own in the fifties and early sixties (Mr. Fender had the Telecaster rolling off the assembly line by 1950), acoustic guitar techniques were still being used. The guitar played background chords while the brass pounded out the heavy riffs that really made the music.

The early history of rock and roll guitar was stifled by this concept. When the electric guitar became popular as a lead instrument for the break in a song, it was toned down and often sounded thin and shallow, especially compared to the saxophone. This is evident from the original Chuck Berry and Buddy Holly records.

It wasn't long before the boys in the garage found out what a volume knob could do. Instead of strumming the chords to the song and singing the melody, guitarists discovered that by cranking up and playing the guitar right in front of the amp facing the speaker that a very peculiar thing happened. The sound was richer and fuller, more sensitive to techniques such as bending and hammering, and most important of all, the notes sustained indefinitely.

The essence of the group became more centered on the six string guitar. A final product of this evolution was the three man rock group. Direction and music power generated by a three instrument group revolves around a single six string guitar. Now the bass and drums work *with* the guitar.

Played Out

You don't have to play at full volume all the time nor are large amps always necessary. A small tube amp and experimentation with sustain devices or a master volume control will provide the elements that you need. My point is this: experience at some point the thrill of playing a guitar that screams with feedback with a single note providing a full, complete sound. I am not suggesting that this is the type of setting that will please everybody for all types of guitarwork, but why not find out what your instrument *is capable of doing*. Once you have played a guitar at this setting and learned to control the oncoming sound, you will understand how a lot of recorded sounds are created. Although most of your guitar playing will take place at a more subdued level, it is a real learning experience to handle a guitar that is feeding back on itself.

96

10•SPEED OF PLAYING

The dexterity of the rock guitarists of the late sixties reached a level that was far greater than the electric guitarists of the 15 previous years. Stars like Hendrix created a whole school of thought that set the precedent for all those who dreamed of real creativity and control. The elements of the rock guitarist became more defined: you had to play fast and clear. There are no short cuts, but there are faster ways to get there.

Speed of playing can be developed over a period of time with the help of conscientious practice of certain exercises. I recommend the various approaches to the blues and the mixed approaches shown in this book. The double triplets and other approaches will increase your flexibility and imprint your mind with *all of the notes* from the scales.

It has always been difficult to pinpoint when and how the learning process takes place. If these scales, approaches and triplets are practiced, even until they seem mechanical and boring, the influence will take place and you will know the right notes before you go to play them. It was in this way that the old blues players were able to play and sing the notes at the same time. This type of familiarity will start to appear in your style in a short time with regular practice.

The most commonly overlooked factor that affects the speed of playing is the action of the pick in the right hand. Almost all of the attention is given to the left hand, but it is the right hand that actually determines the speed of playing. It takes a long time to change deeply ingrained habits that have developed with either hand. Develop the ability to play riffs and scales with an alternate *up and down picking style.* You may find it hard to adapt, but after practice you will see the great advantage in being able to pick using this style.

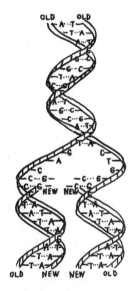

DNA – replication

Two other techniques that increase your speed of playing are the *hammering* on and off of notes and the *pulling* of notes. When you use these methods, it is not necessary to pick each individual note because the left hand actually sounds the notes.

Most of the truly fast and accurate guitar playing we hear, recorded or live, results from the guitarist creating the right conditions. When a tube amp starts to feedback, or with the help of effect devices (master volume control) making the guitar freely sustain, a certain power overtakes the instrument and it becomes very sensitive. Feedback and sustain create a continuum where notes flow from one to the next.

Your guitar neck should be adjusted so the string action is close to the frets and the strings should be thin enough to play and bend easily.

It does not take long to see improvement from intensive practice. The learning curve rises very quickly, especially on a common sense system like the fretboard. The ability to play faster comes like peeling off a strip of tape; it takes twenty seconds to start, and two seconds to peel. If you try until your hand cramps, fretting and sounding each note correctly, the next time out will be easier. Soon enough you will arrive!!!

To increase your speed of playing:
- Practice all of the different approaches (left hand).
- Use an alternate picking style (right hand).
- Adjust neck and strings and let the amp do the work (equipment).

11⁕TEACH YOURSELF

There is one underlying theme that repeatedly surfaces when the great guitarists of rock are asked, how did you learn to play, or who influenced you? In one way or another they all copied other guitarists whom they admired. They developed roots by letting themselves be directly influenced to a certain point during their incubation period until they found their own styles.

You may meet people who will tell you it's not right to copy other artists because it's not original. Don't pay any attention to those people. The best way to teach yourself is by figuring out *exactly how techniques are performed by a variety of artists.* You don't have to duplicate the original when you perform. You just cop the riffs for your own vocabulary. They are really all the same anyway!! Realize that the scales are waiting for you. The greatest thing about copying is the *new input* of techniques which open your eyes to another person's approach to the fretboard.

Eric Clapton copied B.B. King for years before he developed his own idiom with Cream. Keith Richard openly copied Chuck Berry before he went on to write rock history. Hendrix paid his dues in soul bands learning every funky chord there is, while Jimmy Page did his woodshedding with the recordings of Muddy Waters and all those black blues men. There is no exception. They all chose to stand on the shoulders of giants who had already perfected a style and then adapted it to their own medium.

A few decades ago it was not possible, but now you can accelerate the influence factor so you can develop your own style in the direction that you decide. All that you need is a guitar and a tape recorder.

12⁕THE TAPE RECORDER

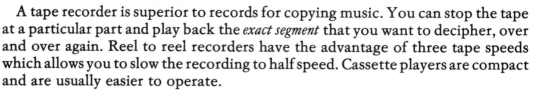

A tape recorder is superior to records for copying music. You can stop the tape at a particular part and play back the *exact segment* that you want to decipher, over and over again. Reel to reel recorders have the advantage of three tape speeds which allows you to slow the recording to half speed. Cassette players are compact and are usually easier to operate.

Fortunately, the recorder that you need for copying music can be of any quality as long as the notes can be heard and identified. Cheap recorders can be obtained through the want ads or in pawn shops. It is far better to have an old or cheap machine that simply works than to spend precious months saving for your dream recorder. My advice: *get one.*

If you do not have access to a complete stereo system with all of the components, buy a portable model with self contained speakers, or a deck model with earphone jacks and there will be no need for other components. Here is the process for learning with the recorder.

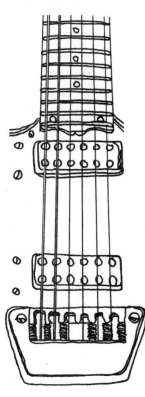

● Tape the lead break to a song where the guitar can be plainly heard. On a reel to reel use the second of the three common speeds (3¾ I.P.S.). If you have several songs that you want to interpret, tape them all in a row noting the numbers on the tape counter. In order to record, run phono plug wires out the back of any

98

good stereo amplifier using the tape out jacks (these jacks often have a predetermined volume level). A standard turntable can be used as a sound source into the amp. This takes surprisingly little time to set up, and after the record is played once you will have it on tape to use indefinitely.

● Tune your guitar to a true scale such as the piano. An acoustic guitar will suffice for practice time with the recorder. Small practice amps at a minimal volume is all that is necessary for the electric.

● Find out the key of the song by figuring out the common chords being used for the opening of the song (refer to chord chart after chapter three). The first chord of a song often has the same letter name as the key.

● Spin the tape up to the beginning of the guitar break and note the number on the tape counter. Listen to the first five or ten seconds of the break over and over again until you are familiar with the notes. Use that rewind button.

Now play the notes to the *Golden Rule* along the root note fret for the song's key. Try to figure out the first few notes of the guitar break. If this is your first time, get ready to sharpen your wits. If you have a reel to reel you can play the riff at half speed (1⅞ I.P.S.) and still be in tune.

Get ready for the lead to work itself out on the patterns we have talked so much about. Remember that you are listening to a finished recording and not an instruction record. It is up to you to figure out which technique was used and how it was executed. At this point, the question of position in the twelve fret scale pattern becomes critical. The root note fret is a good starting point, but remember that most rock guitar leads use *two* five note scales in their construction. It is a sure bet that if you are finding a series of notes particularly difficult to finger, you are in the wrong place. You know how rock guitarists are— they like things *easy*.

Don't be discouraged. My first try took forty-five frustrating minutes to figure out the first twenty seconds of the lead break to *Sunshine of Your Love*. It was worth it. After wondering and faking it for years I could really see what the dude was doing. It was a new game after that. After the recorder has been turned off for an hour and you pick up the guitar, you will have learned.

Watch for rock riffs to appear entirely in the blues scale, entirely in the relative, or combinations of both. The study of how guitarists use the two scales is fascinating and is a large part of breaking down taped music to expose the basics of a guitar style.

Progress will come fast and you will be impressed by the way the recorder can teach. It will soon become evident that the scales are universal for a large cross section of rock music. This fact will hit you head on when you find that the fast overpowering riffs of the real hard rockers use the same boxes as the commercial pop hits.

Betsy

13⊛JAM WITH THE BEST

With the right equipment, you can play your guitar along with any recording from any band, just as if they were in the room with you. The most popular way to do this is to tune up your guitar, find what key the song is in, then play your guitar through your amp with the recording playing through a stereo set.

I have a very effective set up where I run my tape recorder through a separate channel of my amp. First I tape a sequence of songs right after one another. Then I run a stereo male jack out of the stereo earphone plug from the recorder down a line where it is wired into a standard mono jack. This jack is plugged into a separate channel on the guitar amp. The most critical factor is the balance of the volume between the two forces, the recording and your guitar.

I tune my low E string to the bass line of the opening chords of the song, then I turn the recorder off and tune up. Then I put the recording at the desired volume level and slowly bring up the volume of the guitar. I love to jam with the Rolling Stones, Free and Bad Company.

14•LEARN FROM OTHERS

The tape recorder works best with a linear lead guitar style but is lacking when it comes to chord structure and special fingering techniques. You can learn these angles of guitarwork directly from others.

If at all possible, spend time with people that are better than you on the guitar. Go to these people and seek them out. I used to put ads in local college papers saying, "teach me how to play guitar like Hendrix, Page or Clapton." I know there are hundreds of great guitarists but the ad got the point across. The second guy that called said, "You name the song, I'll play it exactly." I said, "Get in tune, I'm coming over immediately." This inevitably led to some all night jams that would never have happened without the ad. Several of the people who responded showed me a few riffs for a few minutes and that helped make the day.

It is important to jam, but it is also important to take a quiet time out so you can concentrate and ask your friend, "How did you do that? Show me exactly." Sometimes spending just ten minutes in this way is more beneficial than spending hours alone. There is something to learn from everybody that plays the guitar. And those people are everywhere.

15•ON IMPROVISING

There are two sides to the world of the electric guitar. One side concerns itself with the material reality of getting the money for good equipment, finding the time to play, getting in tune, finding a place to play, learning the basics and simply finding the energy to get everything together so you can start to make the music happen.

The second side concerns itself with music as an artform. Discussions of art always deal with philosophy, energy, inspiration and the motives that drive the artist to create. Although we are still pretty close to the roots, electric guitar music has a real history of development, an incredible evolution that is still taking place.

Each guitarist that really broke new ground into unexplored territory did so with unbounded energy without care or thought of the past or future. Each trend starter went through personal discovery where he transcended the elements and standards around him and fearlessly did something new.

There is no formula for inspiration, but I think that you can create an atmosphere where it can easily happen. When I first started to learn the five note blues scale, I put small stick-on dots from the stationary store under each note in the scale on the entire fretboard in the key of E. This made it a lot easier to visualize the whole board, with all of its systems. I realized the possibilities were far greater than my small system of habit patterns which were familiar to me. I pushed my lead work from the top through the middle to the bottom in a continuum forcing myself to be indescriminate.

At the very least, I had a better understanding of the discoveries of the great guitarists: a concept that the guitar is a mathematical wavelength machine and the key to improvising is to respect its physical properties. That is simply to know your scale and chord positions and realize that the riff you are playing is a human idea and that you can go right back over the same notes and play a totally different idea. *Never underestimate the familiar.* After you become familiar, the whole thing is downright simple. It gets down to how you hold the note, squeeze the note, stretch the note.

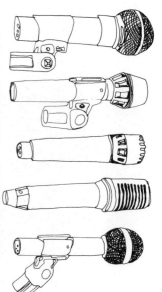

16•OTHER BOOKS

The Harvard Brief Dictionary of Music, Harvard University Press
The Guitar Book, by Tom Wheeler, Harper and Row
The Art and Time of the Guitar from the Hittites to the Hippies, by Frederick Grunfeld, Macmillan
The Guitar Player Book, GPI Publications

The books listed are just a few of my personal favorites but there are dozens more. *The Heavy Guitar Bible* heartily endorses the products of *Guitar Player International Publications. Guitar Player Magazine* has become an industry standard which spotlights the state of the arts. Each month there is an indepth interview with a different professional who makes a living with the old axe. They also have a full line of guitar-related books. Their address is GPI Publications, Box 615, Saratoga, California 95070.

Another great source of guitar-related publications is the *Bold Strummer* in New York City. They have everything and anything that has been written about the guitar. Check them out:156 Fifth Ave. Suite 733, NY, NY 10010.

During the research of this book, I paged through hundreds of books dealing with the guitar from the shelves of libraries. Just go to the card catalogue and look up guitar. They have lots of interesting stuff for free including back issues of *Guitar Player Magazine.* In the Denver public library I found a technique book on Segovia, a history of the guitar and twelve issues of a British rock magazine.

The music dictionary listed above was a great help when it came to writing the chapters on music theory. It is available in paperback and contains a wealth of precise, categorized knowledge.

17 ✺ QUOTES

Jimmy Page, on getting started

"It was 'Baby, let's play house' by Presley. You've got to understand in those days 'rock and roll' was a dirty word. I heard that record and wanted to be part of it. I knew something was going on. The instruments generated so much energy I had to be part of it."

Al DiMeola

"One thing I learned a long time ago was my fretboard, in terms of all the scales in all the positions."

Keith Richard, on getting started

"I'd play whenever I could get my hands on an electric guitar; I was trying to pick up rock and roll riffs and electric blues, the latest of Muddy Waters. I'd spend hours and hours on the same track, back again, and back again."

Herb Ellis, on technical knowledge

"I use all that information, all that knowledge, but it's never done consciously; it's all done intuitively. All I think about is trying to create a melody."

Les Paul

"So in 1934, I asked the Larson Brothers to build me a guitar with a ½" maple top and no f-holes. They thought I was crazy. They told me it wouldn't vibrate. I told them I didn't want it to vibrate, because I was going to put two pickups on it."

Doug Sahm

"I started when I was about six. There was a lady called Aunt Maudie who lived down the street and she had a guitar hanging on the wall. She showed me a few chords."

Gaspar Sanz (1640-1710) from his book on guitar

"Its faults or its perfections lie in whoever plays it, and not in the guitar itself, for I have seen some people accomplish things on one string for which others would need the range of an organ."

Andres Segovia from his autobiography

"My whole being was seized by an indescribable happiness as I began to play the guitar, for its tone was deep and sweet in the bass notes, diaphanous and vibrant in the higher ones. And its accent, the soul of its voice was noble and persuasive. I forgot everything but the guitar..."

Ludwig von Beethoven

"When I open my eyes, I can only sigh, for what I see is contrary to my creed; and I must despise the world for not perceiving that music is a higher revelation than any wisdom or philosophy. It is the wine that inspires new creations, and I am the Bacchus, who presses out this wine for men, and makes them spiritually drunk; when they are sober they bring to shore all kinds of things which they have caught. God is nearer to me than to others. I approach Him without fear, I have always known Him. Neither am I anxious about my music, which no adverse fate can overtake, and which will free him who understands it from the misery which afflicts others."

HEAR THE LIGHT

The Heavy Guitar Bible is designed to be a self-contained system that is whole and complete in book form. In order to complement the knowledge you have gained from the book, The Heavy Guitar Company now announces the availability of six unique products employing an entirely different and dynamic medium: *Cassette Tape Sound Presentations.*

The miracle of tape recording allows us to transcend the problem of communicating the sounds of the guitar by hearing how a technique or passage should actually be played. Each tape package is carefully coordinated with a printed guide.

Our specialty cassette line was developed for the intense six string guitarist who wants to break into a new world of creativity and control over the instrument. All presentations move with a quick precision which include a verbal "hand on guitar" teaching technique with live examples for accelerated learning. Let these tapes teach you a diverse spectrum of fine guitar technique. Now that you know the straight facts from the book, we want you to have a fluid working style.

Not one second of these sixty minute tapes is wasted. Because cassette tapes can be re-wound instantly to playback short segments, each minute is crampacked with fresh new ideas, perfected examples and real sound understanding. You can stop the tape and work with just one concept at a time, just as you would with a teacher. A single thirty second segment may present an idea that you can work on all day.

These tapes are available only through the mail in standard cassette form. We believe that delivery of cassette tapes to your door offers an exceptional way to quickly improve your playing. Thousands of our tape customers around the world agree. We are proud to offer excellent music products and to serve the world's guitarists in such a real and positive way.

THE BIBLE TAPE

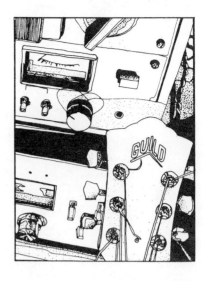

There is a lot of guitarwork between the covers of the Heavy Guitar Bible. The Bible Tape has been created exclusively for use with the book in order to make the pages of the book come live with sound.

The presentation is based on the 88 transcriptions given in the book, all of which are clearly recorded in sequence. However, as each new subject is taken up, the narration drops important pointers and the old gibson cranks out illustrative variations of the spectrum of topics given in the book.

The guitar techniques presented in the book without transcriptions, such as movable chords, harmonics, hammering, sliding, and speed technique are demonstrated along with an overall nutshell review of the lead guitar theory put forth in the book. A printed guide is provided with a new <u>master diagram series</u> which highlights important scale information and can be used for handy reference.

String bending, pulling, octave riffs, triplets, the blues scale, mixed approaches, rhythm riffs, double notes, composite scales, the major scale, playing off the chord, filler notes . . . everything you see in the book, you will hear on the tape, and then some.

BLUES FOREVER

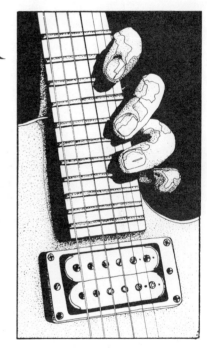

<u>Blues Forever</u> is a one hour soundtrack of blues music made so you can play blues licks, chords, bass lines, harmonica or sing your heart out <u>over the recording</u> until your dues are paid in full! Ever yearn for a bass player that just sticks to the basic structure, or try to find a drummer to keep straight time — nothing fancy? Here they are. You can trust the band to back you up through each and every count of the blues measure, every time through. Their restraint and precision gives you tremendous freedom for improvising, experimenting with phrasing, songwriting and fronting your own band.

Most tracks are twelve bar, but as you move through the numbers, you will find our blues roots to be well researched. There are many interesting varieties of tempo and structure which give special character to all of the individual cuts which include eight-bar blues, the blues turnaround and a lone acoustic number. A graphic guide paper is provided with the tape which breaks down each song to Bar/Chord/Key/Tempo.

More than anything, we know you will have fun with this one. Side One is entirely in the key of A and Side Two is in the key of E. Each side starts with respective tuning fork soundings. Blues Forever just keeps on rolling out the blues one after the other. You will hear lead-ins and some fills, but no melody words or extended lead breaks. That is all left up to you. Riff the blues before work in the morning, pass a harp to a friend and sing your troubles to the red lights on the way there. If you keep turning it over, you can play the <u>Blues Forever.</u>

50 LICKS 1

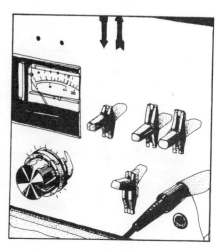

Fifty Licks is a one hour cassette presentation that serves up a full fifty of the heaviest guitar moves you've ever heard. This package is for the rock guitarist who wants his leadwork to have a powerful, dynamic impact.

A unique system is employed in order to communicate the specific information you need to truly understand and play each riff. A technical guidebook is provided which graphically displays all of the diagrams, illustrations and transcriptions used with the tape. Each riff is *explained verbally, transcribed* on the six line staff and clearly *recorded.* Fifty Licks will encourage you in a study of applied lead guitar.

We have set out to capture the different moods of the rock guitar as it is played live on stage. You will learn soaring bent string riffs, movables, full tilt blues, rock and roll chops, lead tricks and some very determined scale climbing. Mix and match and watch your playing grow to new heights in a single playing session.

We feel Fifty Licks is a gold mine for the enthusiast because of the wide range of techniques explored and the high energy with which the riffs are performed.

50 LICKS 2

If you've stayed with us this far, you may be interested in knowing that Fifty Licks 2 is out and it cuts through to fretboard understanding with the same precision as Part 1. Here are 50 more advanced techniques offered to you through clearly transcribed passages. What it boils down to is this: each lick has a unique position, movement, technique and voicing. Some are long, some are short, some are chord workings, repeat moves, sliding over the fret, repeat hammering, right hand on board, sliding octaves, chromatic blues fillers, pinky taps, scat running and going-for-broke blues bends. By applying these new riffs to your present vocabulary, you will experience accelerated development.

ROCK RHYTHMS

This tape is designed for those who want to play lead guitar with a rhythm player that will push you on to new musical heights. Recorded for your improvising pleasure are a series of twelve rhythm guitar tracks which will take you on to a musical journey all the way from slow tempo minor chord turnarounds to power chord jamming. Each track has its own special texture and feeling, but all were designed to feature you on lead guitar.

Before the session on side one begins, tape commentary will vividly explain the chord changes and the structure of each jam including the song's key, chord positions, tempo, how the bridge works and hints on how to apply lead guitar patterns over the recording.

Best of all, Rock Rhythms will never let you down. Here is driving rock and roll at your fingertips. When problems with equipment and meeting people make things a bit too complicated . . . just slip on the cassette and you are ready to break free. Put it through the stereo at a good volume level and you can tune up the electric and take off. Practice scales on your acoustic guitar while the tape is playing through a smaller portable unit.

We bet you find yourself playing the tape's driving rhythms over and over again, as you turn all of the theory you have studied into real creative improvising.

POWER CHORD SECRETS

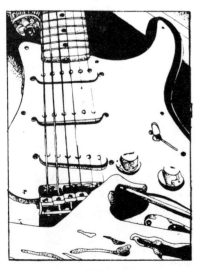

The secret to good power chording is knowing how, where and when to go for the chord position that is going to give you the right sound. Here is a close look into how chords are used together, the possibilities for the movement of the left hand, the role of the right hand, quick switchovers, tap-ons and common chord sequence. Included in this study will be exhaustive step-by-step exercises using major, minor and seventh chords which cover the entire territory of the fretboard from top to bottom, thick to thin.

Power chords are not strummed to the rhythm of a song, but work closely with the drums to provide a strong energy pulse which is the trademark of electric rock. We picked apart a lot of great records in order to get the overall picture of how these special chords are utilized and we found certain moves used over and over again. Using practice examples, Power Chord Secrets will provide you with a working guide to these universal chord applications.